Learning About Dogs

Click

for Grooming

handling and treatment

Karen McCarthy

A LEVEL 2 Book
CLICKER TRAINERS
COURSE

Printed in the U.S. and distributed by
Karen Pryor ClickerTraining and Sunshine Books
49 River Street, Waltham, MA 02453
www.clickertraining.com
Sales: U.S. Toll Free 800-472-5425
781-398-0754

First published in 2006

Learning About Dogs Limited

PO Box 13, Chipping Campden, Glos, GL55 6WX. UK

cover picture of Vienna by Damon Standish

ISBN 1-890948-31-4

Books in the Clicker Trainers Course series by Kay Laurence:

- Clicker Foundation Trainer Level 1
- Clicker Novice Trainer Level 2
- Clicker Intermediate Trainer Level 3

Recipe books for specialised interests to progress from Level 2

- Clicker World Competition Obedience
- Clicker Dances with Dogs
- Clicker Ringcraft
- Clicker Gundog

Clicker Agility for Fun and Fitness by Diana Bird

Teaching Dogs Magazine for up-to-date news on clicker training

www.clickertraining.com

CONTENTS

1 Introduction

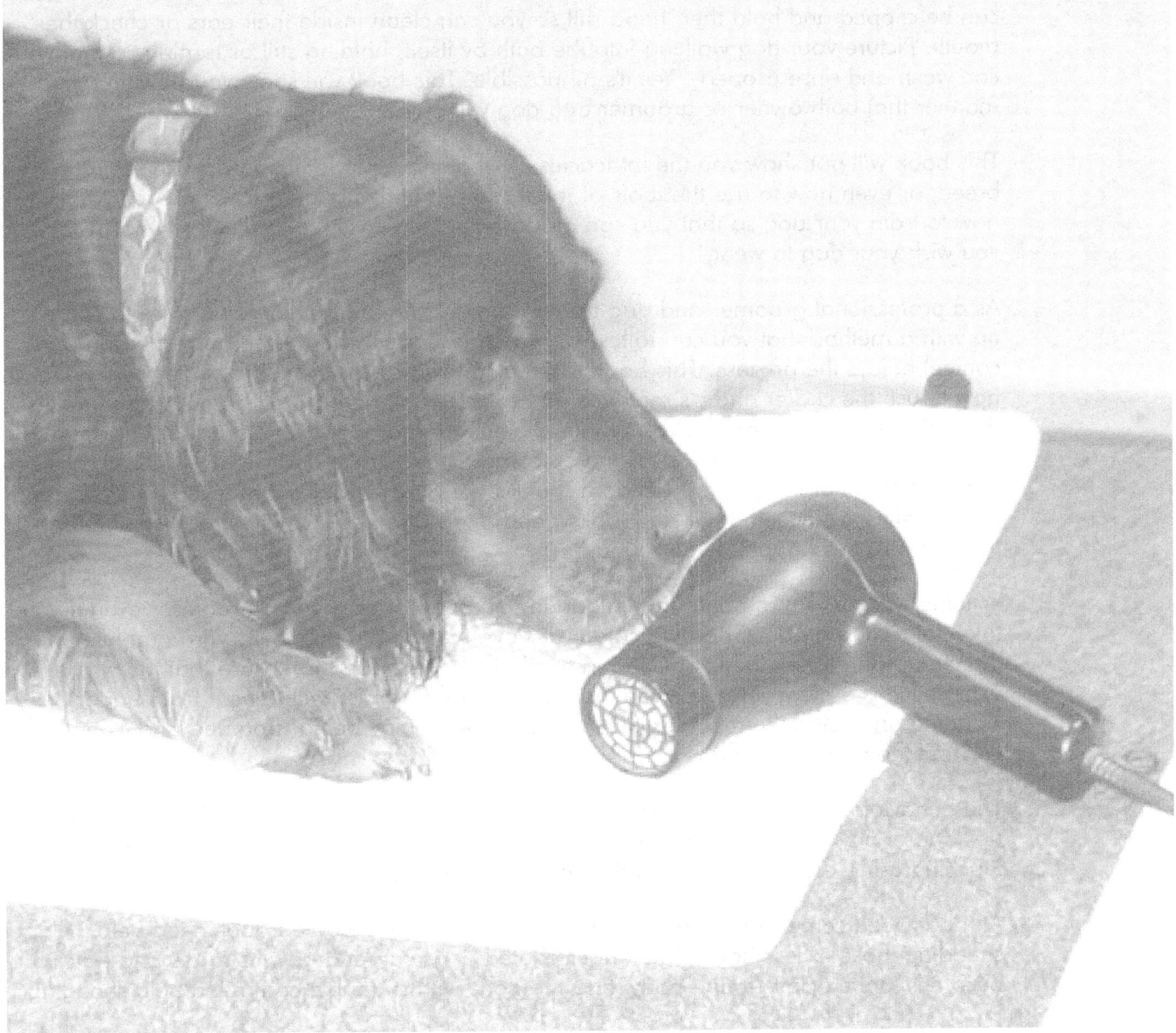

- Do you enjoy bathing or grooming your dog?
- Does your dog enjoy it?
- Does bathing or grooming your dog become a marathon session that has to be planned for in advance?
- Want to learn how to teach your dog to enjoy the entire process instead of bathing and grooming being a more challenging experience for both of you?

Imagine being able to ask your dog to look up so that you can brush their neck. Have them turn one way or the other so you can brush both sides, offer you a foot so the nails can be clipped and hold their head still so you can clean inside their ears or check their mouth. Picture your dog walking into the bath by itself, holding still or turning so that you can wash and rinse properly. Yes it's all possible. This book will show you how, in a manner that both owner or groomer and dog will enjoy.

This book will not show you the intricacies of what clip or style is appropriate for your breed, or even how to use the tools of the trade. What this book hopes to teach you is how to train your dog so that you can groom your dog easily regardless of what style you wish your dog to wear.

As a professional groomer and dog trainer I have been able to combine roles to come up with a method that you can follow for grooming dogs where everybody (human and canine) enjoys the process. This book is directed towards teaching the owner or groomer how to use the clicker and it's methods, in order to make grooming an enjoyable process for both dog and caregiver alike. Small or big, young or old, every dog that I have groomed, or seen groomed, loves the outcome. They prance and run around with a renewed sense of invigorated freedom. But it's not only the dog's that love it, the owners too are always pleased, their dog looks good, feels good and smells great - a combination that inspires happiness all round.

Whether you groom at home in the lounge, the bedroom or the bathroom or even if you take the dog to a dog-grooming salon, or have the salon come to you (in a mobile unit), the clicker and it's methods outlined in this book can be used to ensure that the whole experience is a pleasant one. Even the professional groomer will benefit from understanding and using the methods outlined. Dogs will enjoy being groomed and owners will find the process rewarding.

The behaviours shown here for grooming can also be used for your dog's medical check-ups and at anytime the dog needs to be examined. And once you've learned the art of teaching using a clicker, your imagination becomes endless.

All dogs need some form of grooming. Yes, even the short coated dogs need help shedding those excess hairs. The longer coated dogs can end up with knots and hair that becomes matted close to the body, and the dogs with a double coat need help shedding during Spring. Grooming helps you keep a close eye on your dog's body, and gives you the skills of being able to identify any changes that may occur. A mentally happy and physically healthy dog performs any request willingly and in a confident and joyful manner; and if a dog is happy and confident then the owner will be too.

By using the clicker hand in hand with the training recipes outlined in this book, the behaviours required become solid, the dog becomes a much more willing student and active worker which make further behaviours easier to teach. Using the clicker gives both the human and the canine a concise and clear interpretation of the information being relayed.

In this book I've concentrated on grooming within the home environment, but have also included an extra section for those working in the pet-grooming salon where other people's pets are being groomed.

The book assumes you have the basic clicker training skills as detailed in the Foundation Book of the Clicker Trainers Series by Kay Laurence. You should understand how the clicker works, use different rewards, be able to add a cue, use basic shaping and teach targeting. If you become more interested in clicker training then you can follow the course through the Novice and Intermediate books.

You should have taught your dog to sit, stand, down, and stay or wait on cue.

I've also included some comments on basic canine learning behaviour so that the reader can understand why some dogs have yet to learn the enjoyment of being groomed, and why some seem to be the perfect pooches when the brush comes out, or the bath is run.

Each training recipe shows step by step how the dog and handler achieve the desired result. However as the trainer you may need to be ready to advance quite quickly through the steps, as it is also dependent on how clicker savvy your student is and how much relearning they are doing in the grooming department. Some dogs will advance quickly while others need more time gaining the understanding of what you are teaching. I have found that it does not matter what breed or type of dog you are teaching, but that the rate of learning is a direct result of the trainer's ability combined with the historical experience for the dog being groomed.

LEARNED BEHAVIOUR

Unless it's a natural canine behaviour, dogs and puppies offer behaviours and react to situations in our society because a human has reinforced them to behave that way. Dogs are born wanting to learn and unfortunately it is often the human intervention that teaches them to fear and be defensive. It is our teaching that can set a dog up for life in many situations.

If you set the dog up in a secure environment and introduce a new stimulus in such a way that the dog is able to offer a certain behaviour, the dog will generally repeat that behaviour if it is confident and rewarding the first time that they encounter a situation.

If however the situation is frightening or forced, the dog or puppy will not learn a positive association and may either shut down their activity (which includes the learning aspect) or could in a dire case, lash out in defence - this is unfortunately often mistaken as the dog being aggressive when in fact it was forced into a situation where it's natural defensive mechanism was switched on.

For grooming purposes experienced dogs also learn the same way as puppies but they may have already learned that fidgeting and yelling during a grooming session ends the session enabling them to do more rewarding activities.

It is much easier, and I must say a whole lot more pleasant, to be able to teach a dog to become a willing partner in any process that you may ask them to encounter. This willingness is captured and enhanced using positive reinforcement techniques. For some people it is easier just to force a situation to occur. I believe that it is fundamentally much more influential to have an ally that willingly wishes to be a part of your life rather than be forced to be there.

To use the clicker effectively is a challenge in itself, but one that continues to give so much more satisfaction than not using it.

THE CLICKER

Why does the clicker work better than using just positive reinforcement?

Basically it's all about timing and reward. Timing a click is much more accurate than timing verbal or physical praise, and pairing it with a reward gives the click meaning. The dog moves so quickly that being able to use the clicker ensures that we are marking and rewarding the exact movement that is required. Training is also cut down to a minimum, which ensures it is kept fun and interesting.

I have actually seen some of the recipes in this book used where the groomer has decided not to use the clicker to mark the behaviour and used just positive reinforcement. It worked. A dog that was petrified of nail clipping was taught to offer its paw in confidence to have the nails clipped. With training 2-3 times per week it took about 5 months. Using the clicker and the same number of training sessions took 2 weeks, with each training session only lasting 2-3 minutes, and remember the dogs were absolutely petrified of having their nails clipped. A dog that is confident and trusting understands the behaviour in only 2-3 sessions, depending on the ability of the trainer and the motivation used of course.

The clicker's success is also in its ability to remain consistent, in tone and application. Research is now indicating that because of this consistency of acoustic tone that this creates an acoustical binary message which is processed by the brain quickly and speeds up muscle learning. Therefore the muscles that perform the movement of the body for taught behaviour are gaining a type of memory of their own. Therefore using the clicker creates a more precise, reliable body movement or behaviour.

LURING

Many of the behaviours and actions that we require in grooming are very specific, due to the groomer wanting to ensure the dog remains consistent while using sharp instruments that could injure if used incorrectly. So some of the recipes use luring to start the behaviour; the luring could be in the form of using the reward itself or training a target or hand touch to show the dog what is required.

However there is no reason why both shaping and capturing the behaviours cannot work to begin the behaviour, the trainer just needs to make sure that they plan the training carefully, and it does help to have a dog that understands what the click means. Luring can also occur by subtle body movements of our own, so wherever practicable ensure that your own body language remains consistent throughout the training and subsequent grooming.

SHAPING

The art of using shaping to build a required behaviour gives the dog a type of control over what it is being asked to do. This control will give the dog the confidence to perform the task willingly and accurately, which as said before is of the utmost importance when using sharp equipment in precarious places. We can use shaping to encourage the dog into and out of the bath, (Although out of the bath doesn't generally need any encouragement!), or up steps onto a bench, to turn slightly or all the way round, and to commonly encourage the dog to make that extra effort that we may want.

Shaping also teaches the dog how to remember what to do, they become very self aware and mentally engaged in the interaction.

PHYSICAL MANIPULATION

Although clicker training is usually a hands off training, grooming of course is very much hands on. It therefore becomes important to learn how to physically manipulate the dog properly so that it is comfortable and to also use the clicker at the same time, without resorting to needing 3 pairs of hands to do this.

Tip

Always let the dog know you are about to touch them and let them feel where your hand is going. ie: if you are about to pick up a foot, run your hand down the dog's back, and then down the leg to the foot.

There is a myriad of books available that can tell you exactly which muscles move which part of the body and it could be a good idea to have a greater understanding so that you don't inadvertently do damage while manipulating the dog physically. However most of the time the dog will tell you if what you are doing or about to do is uncomfortable. It's one of the wonderful things about most dogs - they sure do let you know when something isn't right - it's only a matter of experience on our behalf to understand what the dog is saying.

Dogs are built differently and age takes its toll on the body, so always respect how the body works and how the dog is feeling, ensuring their comfort is a top priority.

When touching the dog ensure your body posture is relaxed and that you do not become over-bearing by bending over the dog, which could instigate a vulnerability fear from the dog. It may be necessary to crouch down beside the dog when attempting some of these exercises. As you touch each area, name it as the dog will learn to associate that particular naming sound with the area on it's body which will be helpful in the future.

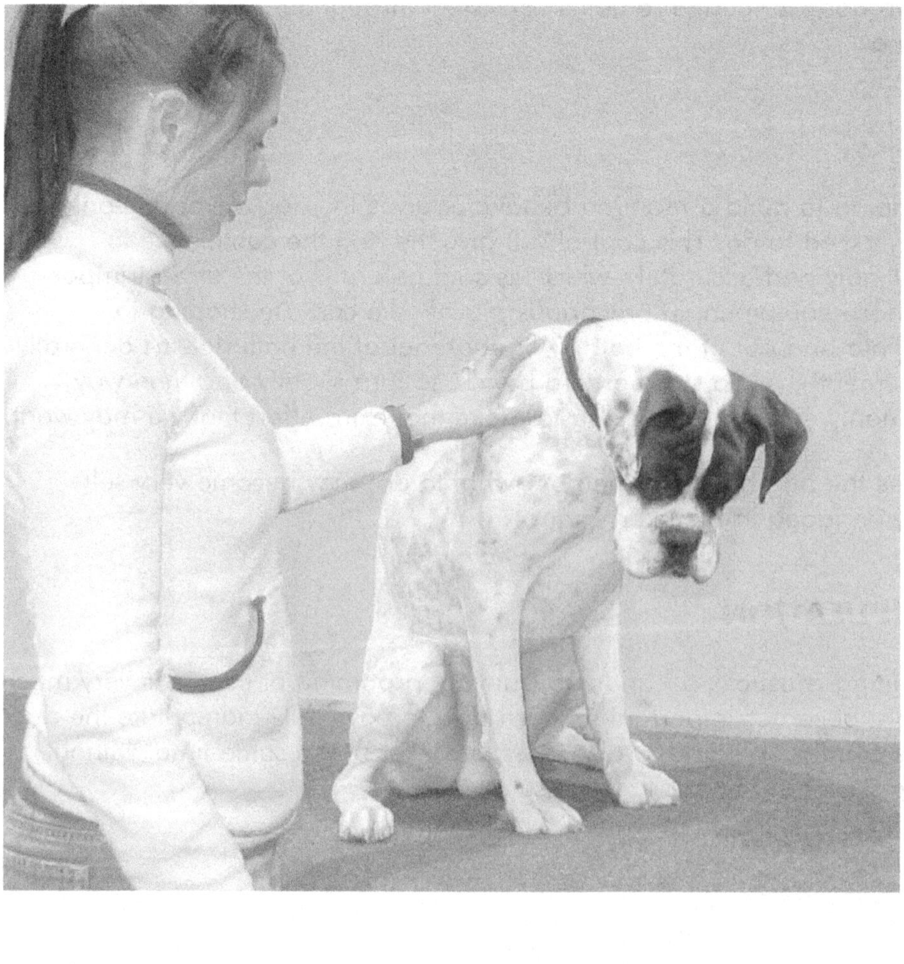

learn to touch your dog with empathy

TARGETING

With targeting you can teach a dog to go to an object so that it positions itself in a manner that you can use for grooming ease. A dog can overcome a fear of apparatus or environments by building on where or what a target is.

Common targets in the grooming environment are the different surfaces and apparatus, i.e. target the bath, the bench, the floor or a wall. Using towels, rubber mats, markers or boxes or similar can take the dog on a journey to the required place. Being able to move small targets up and down the wall for nose touching can help keep the head at the right height. Even the use of toys can become targets - go fetch the rubber duck in the bath, place your foot on the ball without rolling it, stand still on the step or the box. Your imagination can run wild when you begin using targets and any environment can contain the most unusual apparatus, i.e. a flower pot turned upside down for keeping the foot on, or even up the right way for keeping one foot in so you can touch another foot without fidgeting occurring.

Target sticks are also great for luring behaviour like turning around or go to this spot, without the need for the groomer to always be in front of the dog.

IMPORTANCE OF GROOMING YOUR DOG

Grooming your dog is not only beneficial to his health but also to the whole human and canine relationship. A healthy dog is happy and confident and these dogs get attention from their human counterpart, which in turn is more likely to ensure they have appropriate manners in other parts of their life.

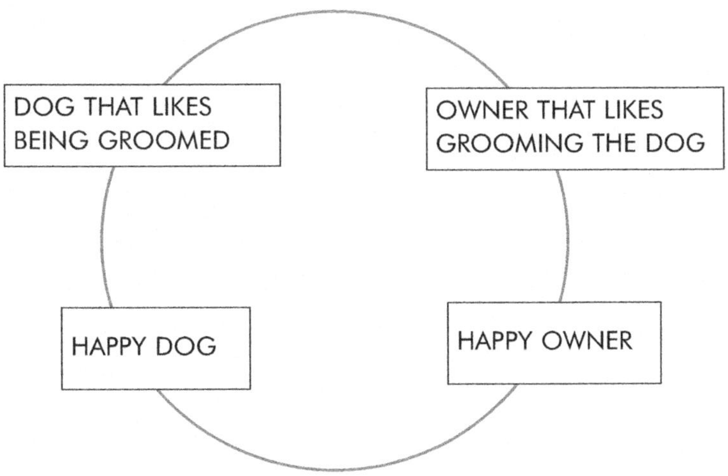

The act of grooming itself removes the dead hair and skin from the coat and spreads the natural oils over the body that in turn help eradicate any unpleasant odours. For long coated dogs brushing and combing the coat separates the hair and allows the skin to breathe. Tangles and matted areas of coat can be quickly dealt with and only occur minimally if grooming is regular. Unfortunately when tangles occur they can quickly turn into bigger tangles or matted hair and this prevents the skin from breathing as well as causing a build up of the skin's oils beneath these areas. Sores can appear on irritated skin and these sores can end up causing pain and/or discomfort to the dog, an unpleasant odour and perhaps even veterinary attention.

Apart from medical attention being required if a dog hasn't been groomed regularly retention of a long coat will mean many hours of grooming and probably lots of pain and discomfort to the dog in trying to get the tangles and matted hair out. In severe cases the whole coat can be matted which will inhibit free movement for the dog. Any of these aspects can lead to an uncomfortable and irritable dog.

But not only that it also means that generally the dogs coat will have to be clipped very short (almost to the skin) and grown again - not necessarily a pleasant experience for the dog in colder climates. However at least then the art of grooming can be re-learned as the coat is being grown.

There are also many researched health benefits to Humans that happen while they are grooming their dogs. Both humans and dogs need tactile contact in order to live a full, balanced and subsequently healthy life. Enjoying the grooming process means that both species get some physical touch, and this touching helps reduce stress which can help lower blood pressure, which in turn helps reduce heart disease.

Before we delve into how to groom your dog easily we also need to know a little bit about the equipment required and how to use the environment successfully.

2 Grooming

GROOMING EQUIPMENT

UTENSILS

It is important to use the correct tools when grooming your dog, you can check with the dog's breeder or ask your local veterinary clinic or pet shop for advice on what tools are best for your dog's coat, or even more ideally ask someone at the local dog grooming parlour.

Most tools are designed to make the task easier on both the dog and on the person on the other end of the brush. Although it can be tempting to just get one brush or comb that seems to have a multitude of uses, these type of utensils are often only really good for a limited use, and because of this can turn what is essentially an easy job into a more difficult one and thus end the task of grooming. So buying a reasonable quality of tool that will last a lot longer, if not a lifetime will make the job easier and ensure that the task of grooming your dog continues on a regular basis.

The brand of tool is essentially a personal choice, however ask if you can see one in use and maybe even ask to test a variety for weight and comfort. Sometimes asking other owners of similar coated dogs what they use and comparing notes will give a better knowledge for decision.

Whatever tools you decide to use on a dog, let the dog familiarise itself with the item before you use it. Dogs are naturally curious animals and this simple act of showing the dog the tool and letting it take a sniff can often help the dog settle into the routine of being groomed. Whenever I groom a dog, and especially a new client, I will always let the dog watch what I am doing, look at what I am holding and have a good sniff of it if they are interested. There's nothing scarier than having something put on your body that you are unfamiliar with, I wouldn't expect to like it myself so I don't expect a dog to either.

SOFT BRISTLE BRUSH (A) General soft brush that is not only great for teaching new dogs to enjoy the process of brushing, but also for longer coated dogs with single layer coats.

RUBBER BRISTLE BRUSH (B) Soft firm rubberised brush that helps dogs shed their coats. Brilliant for short-coated dogs.

FLEA COMB (C) Removes fleas and flea husks from the dog's coat. Great for knot free coats.

SLICKER BRUSH (D) Soft wire bristle helps smooth out small tangles in fine hair, fluff up silky hair and helps remove undercoat from double-coated dogs.

RUBBER GROOMING GLOVE (E) Same implement as the rubber bristle brush but is worn on the hand for ease of use, can have suede on back for hair polishing.

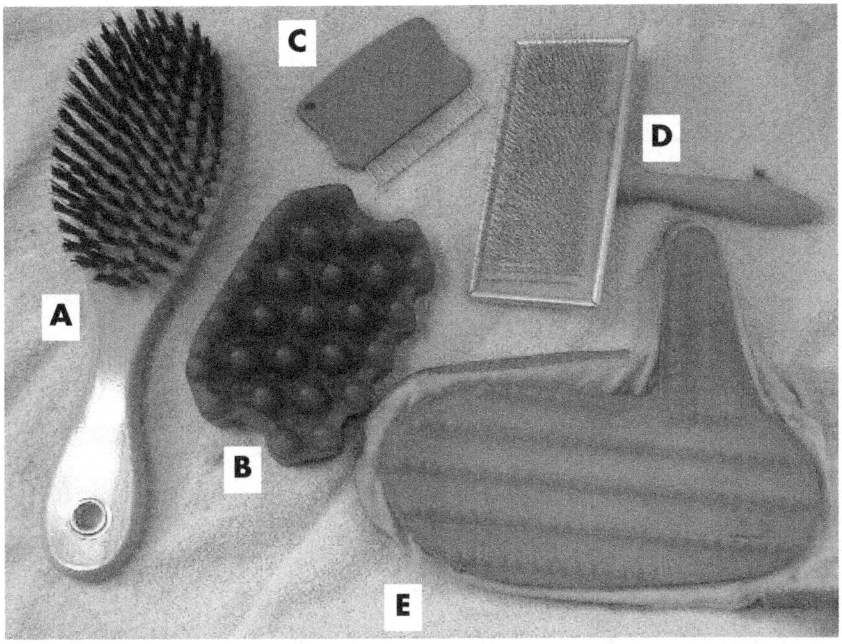

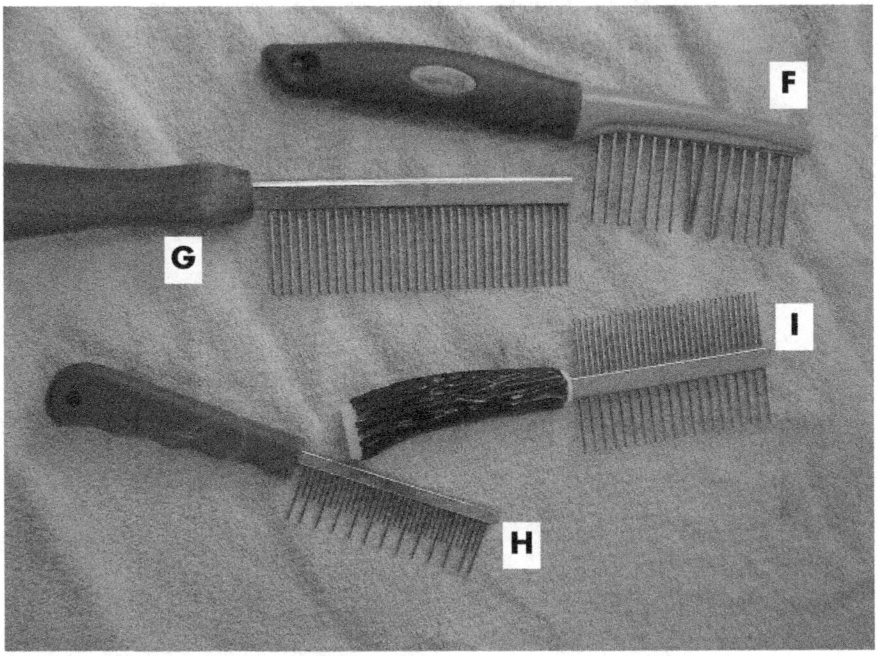

WIDE TOOTH COMB (F) Perfect for long dense coats, comb teeth are able to work through entire coat from hair surface down to skin.

NARROW TOOTH COMB (G) Great for ensuring no tangles or knots remain in coats. Wonderful is used after the wide-tooth comb.

DOUBLE TOOTH COMB (H) Has the benefit of reaching closer to the skin while keeping the outer layer free from knots.

DOUBLE SIDED COMB (I) Gives the option of narrow and wider teeth spacing in one implement.

DE-MATTING COMB (J) Brilliant for cutting through matted hair. Used in a sawing motion through hair so as not to pull the knot out.

UNDERCOAT RAKE (K) Great for dogs with double coats, used more during the spring or other times when the dog is moulting.

STRIPPING KNIFE (L) Used to strip any dead hair from the coat.

STRIPPING BRUSH/COMB (M) Also used to strip dead hair from the coat but is used in a brushing motion.

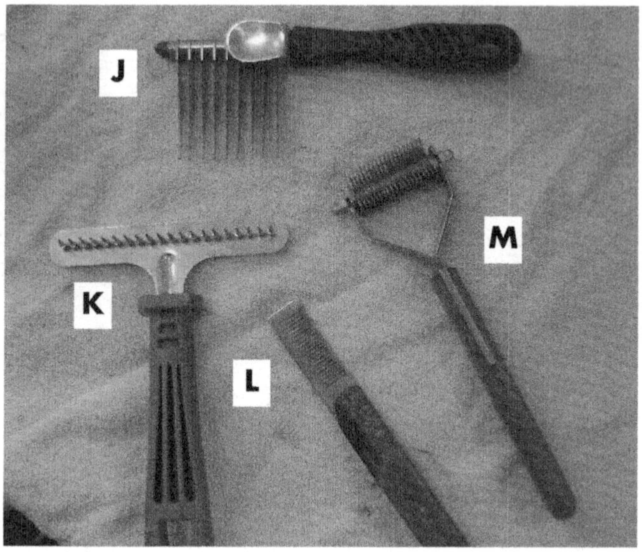

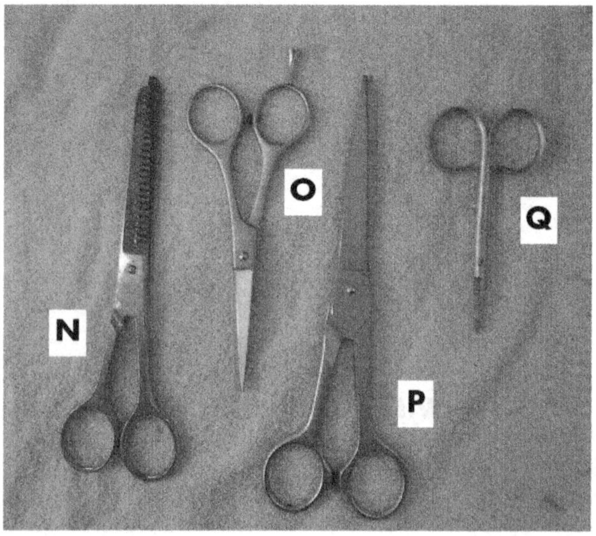

THINNING SCISSORS (N) Removes bulky hair without showing scissor marks in coat.

SMALL-POINT SCISSORS (O) Handy for trimming hair in harder to reach areas.

8" SCISSORS (P) Perfect for trimming longer areas evenly

EAR PLUCKING SCISSORS (Q) Required for dogs whose coats don't shed but where hair continues to grow.

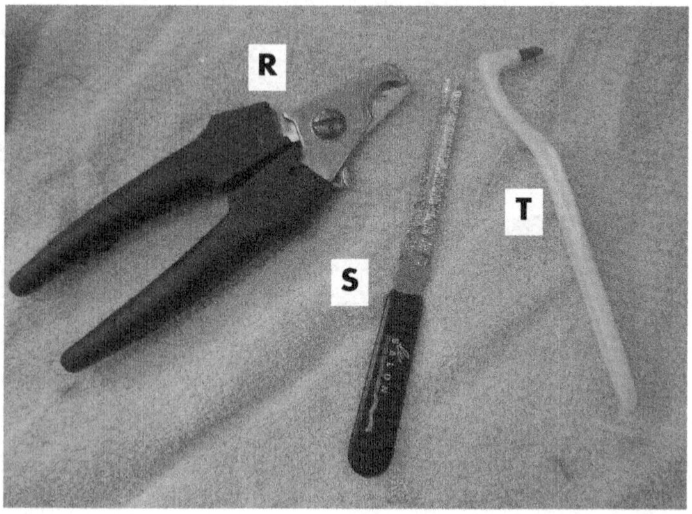

NAIL CLIPPERS (R) Heavy duty scissor specially designed for cutting dog nails.

NAIL FILE (S) Removes the sharp edges that nail clippers can sometimes leave behind/

TOOTH SCALER (T) Used to help reduce tartar buildup in a dog's mouth.

OTHER HELPFUL TOOLS

- Bath mat or similar to reduce the risk of your dog slipping on a wet surface. Using a towel in the bottom of the bath or shower can also help, as well as using a slightly damp towel for grip on the grooming surface.
- Targets to stand on - a book, folded newspaper, magazine, computer mouse pad, piece of carpet or cardboard or anything of a similar type can be used as a visual aid for targeting the dog.
- Other targets - toys in the bath or on the bench, distraction toys that keep the dog relatively still but busily distracted.
- Clicker board - this is a clicker that you can use under foot, which enables you to click while leaving your hands free. Alternatively you can add a strap to it and position it anywhere on your body - be careful that you are fully in control of the click though and also able to react with perfect timing.
- Treat pouch or similar container. The treat container needs to be within reach, sealed but able to be quickly opened or within reach of you but out of reach of the dog.
- Somewhere to put your tools where they are easily accessible but not able to be kicked off the bench by the dog.
- A hand held shower attachment. This can be very handy for mixing water and ensuring the dog becomes thoroughly wet and rinsed off after shampooing.

FACILITIES

Many of us only have a bathroom or the outside garden in which to bath our dogs, but I have seen homes that have areas specially built for bathing their dogs. Whichever you choose to have it is important to make sure that when you bath the dog, that safety for both yourself and the dog is paramount but spare a thought to setup so that perhaps a minimal amount of mess can be left that has to be cleaned up.

Things to think about regardless of what facilities you have or use:

- Availability to water (preferably warm)
- Ease of getting dog into and out of bathing vessel
- Non-slip flooring in bathing vessel

- Ease of keeping dog in grooming area
- Ease of cleaning any mess likely to be left after bathing or grooming. Grooming over wooden floors or linoleum type surfaces is easier to clean up than over carpet or other fabrics.
- Closeness to electrical sockets (properly power surge protected) if using a hair dryer, clippers or other electrical equipment.
- Ability to groom dog comfortably at a sensible height - nothing worse than having to bend over the dog or reach up to it all the time during grooming sessions.

WATER TEMPERATURE

It is important to use warm water when bathing your dog in readiness for brushing or combing. Just like our hair and skin, the skin's pores open with the warmth and close with the cold. The use of warm water will help excess hair to be removed more easily as the skin's pores will open. Dogs have nerves that feel temperature changes, and just as water that is too hot will burn, water that is too cold will cause the dog's body temperature to drop below a healthy level. If we want grooming to be as pleasant as possible, then ensuring the dog's comfort throughout the whole process will aid in this goal.

Many people believe that it is fine to douse the dog with the garden hose. In my experience this can lead to a dog becoming frightened of the hose and stressing unnecessarily whenever someone holds a hose, even if it is not directed at the dog. Some dogs may play with the water from the hose and these dogs are generally confident, happy and healthy dogs, but there is a wide chasm of difference between play and forcefulness. Using an outside garden hose in cooler climates will cause the dog to be cold throughout the process. If you use a garden hose in hot climates you will need to let the water run for a few minutes first to ensure that you don't use the first water from the hose as the water remaining in the hose from the last use may have heated up with the sun.

Even if you always wash your dog in the bathroom or a purpose-built facility, there can be times when you may need to wash them down outside - I know Vienna and Connor quite happily roll in smells that I deem unpleasant and that could be something I don't want anywhere near the inside of home!

RECIPE 1

HOSING THE DOG

To be able to train a dog to at least tolerate if not enjoy being hosed in the garden, trust of the handler for the dog is imperative. A clicker trained dog will quite happily accept being hosed in the garden and the process will leave only positive effects. Follow the steps below to help a dog become accustomed to and enjoying being hosed.

Have fun with the dog and relax during the training, try not to rush this process so that the dog can spend many future years enjoying being hosed if that is the way in which your dog is to be washed.

1. With the dog outdoors near the hose, click the dog for movement towards the hose, which is currently turned off. Repeat 3-4 times.
2. Progress to the dog actually touching the hose and then raise the criteria for maintaining a longer touch of the hose.
3. Repeat steps 1and 2 with the hose turned on low, then repeat again with the hose turned on higher.
4. Try it with you holding the hose, first turned off, and then on low and then on a higher pressure.

5. Go right back to the beginning steps with the water gently dripping on the dog. Click and treat frequently to ensure the position of standing is maintained during the hosing.
6. Increase the water pressure and move over the dog, expect the dog to have a shake during the process - this is normal doggy behaviour.
7. Keep bringing the dog back to position and click, treating for standing still during the process.

An alternative is to have the dog touch a target and maintain that hold while you wet them down, however I prefer to have the dog interacting with me during the process.

GROOMING MYTHS

HOW OFTEN SHOULD YOU BATH THE DOG?

I've seen dogs that have never had a bath in their life to ones that are bathed on a very regular basis. In today's society dogs are living more and more often inside our homes, sleeping in the same room and many get the luxury of even sharing the same bed. A clean, fresh smelling dog gets more rewards and privileges. They get more pats and cuddles and more attention from not only the immediate family but from many friends and visitors. I've seen dogs that are not allowed inside if they smell and ones that have their feet regularly bathed before being allowed to step over the threshold.

I've yet to come across an animal caregiver that wasn't happy that their dog was clean. Perhaps many years ago when dogs were being housed outside like other stock, there was a need not to bathe them too often, perhaps the shampoos were not designed with the pet's coat in mind. Today we are lucky that there is a wide array of products that we can use that will help keep our furry friends smelling sweet. However that's not to say that the natural odour of the dog is not a sweet smell, but each of us has a different sense of smell and what is odorous to one is perhaps not that pungent to another.

I've weighed up the pros and cons of bathing a dog frequently and taken special note of those dogs I see regularly on a professional basis and also those I see infrequently, in order to determine a realistic opinion of frequent bathing. Apart from the process taking up a little bit more time in the year, the benefits far outweigh any perceived disadvantages. Everyone is happier when the dog is clean and smelling good, and that can only be beneficial to the dog's temperament because when the household is happy the dog is also happy. And a happy dog is generally a confident one that can deal with new situations with ease, so this in turn is good for the dog's success within our every increasing rules of acceptable behaviour in society.

The dogs that I bathe on a weekly basis have better coats and rarely develop skin problems, or at least not related to the bathing process. Interestingly enough if your dog does develop skin problems, the most frequent advice I hear is the dog needs to be bathed weekly using a medicated shampoo, and that mainly comes recommended from the veterinary profession, but you only need to read the medicated shampoo bottles to verify it. Apart from smelling good and helping keep the skin clean, frequent bathing will also help detect any lumps, bumps or scratches early enough to be dealt with quickly. And when a positive event occurs with regularity the whole temperament of the dog can change from any perceived fear or apprehension of the process to actually looking forward to and enjoying the recurrent bathing session.

CLIPPING OR TRIMMING HAIR

Dogs come in all shapes and sizes and so does their texture and thickness of hair. We've managed to breed dogs that shed excessively, ones that don't shed at all and even dogs without any hair.

Tools used to clip or trim hair range from a variety of types and sizes and include scissors through to electric clippers. It is important that the operators of either scissors or electric clippers are thoroughly trained on the proper use and care, there are plenty of books and other manuals available that can help with this. The different tools that are used in grooming can be quite scary to a dog because of the noise they make and the feel of them on their coat and skin. Clippers can be loud and they also vibrate which can be quite daunting as it is a feeling that is foreign to a dog, but even the noise of the scissors working can be nerve racking, especially close to sensitive areas like the head and pelvic region. Just like us the dogs are fully aware of their body parts and of how close we get to them.

There are a couple of ways of introducing the dog to all sorts of tools using the clicker:

- to get the dog to interact with the item and
- allow the dog to concentrate on something else while the tool is being used

I have found that a combination of both ways is important and that even more important is the confidence of the person using the equipment. What is wonderful and very useful is that using the clicker gives the dog the confidence of coping with new and potentially stressful situations. If the introduction of a new object or situation is paired with behaviour offering using the clicker, the dog is able to generalise better.

Getting the dog to interact with the equipment is a great way of allowing the dog to overcome any fear of electrical or mechanical devices.

allowing the dog to interact with new objects can remove the fear

RECIPE 2

WHAT'S THAT?

introducing equipment and tools

1. Without the distraction of anything else, put the tool on the floor or hold it in your hand but away from your body. Natural curiosity should overtake the dog to at least look or glance at the object. Click for even mild interest.

   Where you put the tool is dependent on what tool you are introducing, if the tool is likely to get damaged or is too dangerous for the dog to start play interacting with, then you need to control the object.

   If the dog does not look at the tool in any way, then you may need to check where you are in relation to the tool, try putting it between you and the dog so the dog has to at least pass by it in order to get to you. At the passing by point, click.

2. When the dog is actively looking at the object, withhold the click to create more interest and then click for more interaction.

   At this point the dog may get a little frustrated because it is not being clicked for just looking or glancing at the object and this frustration should create a greater interest which is what you want to capture.

3. You could continue to raise the criteria and create a retrieve of the tool, but again this depends on the tool as to whether you would want to risk it being dropped, marked by teeth or even slobbered on.

The next important step is to handle the equipment around the dog. If the dog becomes nervous when you are holding the equipment teaching the retrieve is very useful. Even without the retrieve holding the equipment and getting the dog to perform another behaviour that has no relation to the tool will help the dog not be concerned about what you have in your hand.

It is important that you do this with noisy equipment like clippers and hairdryers. Once the dog is comfortable around the tools, try turning the tools on, to the lowest power and noise level possible and ensure that it is facing away from the dog when it is turned on. Do not make an issue of interacting with the equipment but do something else with the dog that it is happy with.

Once the dog is not worried about the noise of the equipment then it is time to move the equipment over the dog. Turn the tools off, hold them in your hand and move them around the dog without actually touching the dog, click and treat the dog for targeting or looking away from the equipment - i.e. for anything that doesn't incorporate worrying about the gear. Then turn the equipment back on while it is facing away from the dog

Dog offers a clicker trained behaviour, whilst the hair dryer is switched on but out of sight behind the back

and slowly begin to move it around the dog's body, remember your body language needs to be easy and casual in order to let the dog believe that nothing untoward is happening or about to happen.

This is where it can be handy to use a foot clicker so that you can continue to click and treat the dog while also using the equipment.

Another method is to teach the dog to ignore what is happening to it and concentrate on another behaviour. Generally the best behaviour is to target something with the nose that is close to the dog so that it doesn't have to move in order to be clicked and treated.

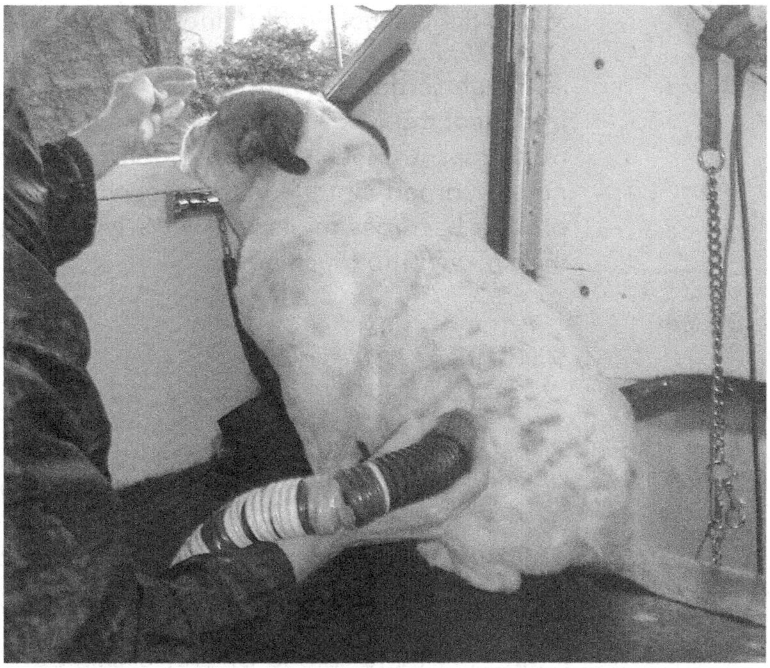

The dog is focused on the treat out of the window, whilst the dryer in switched on.

APPLYING GROOMING TO THE DIFFERENT DOGS

PUPPIES AND FIRST TIMERS

With some dogs, due mainly to the type of coat they have, first time grooming may not happen until they are well into the first year of age or more. Because of the way canines learn, it is important that, regardless of breed, all dogs learn how pleasant being groomed can be. Even though some breeds have long coats as adults many of them may have very short ones as a puppy, and despite having long hair the coats of most breeds stay fairly tangle free for quite a number of months as a puppy, which in turn can lead to the dog not get used to being groomed until they are much older.

As a professional groomer I often get the chance to teach dogs right from the beginning that being groomed is a wonderful experience. With puppies it is important to take the time to play with them and let them experience the tools that are used in a positive manner. A puppy looks to you for guidance on how to respond to what is happening so careful but fun management of the first grooming lesson will set them up confidently for a lifetime of hair and skin care.

It is much more pleasant to groom a dog that enjoys the process than one that has learnt that grooming is a time of painful coat pulling, physical manipulation and associated with their owner getting frustrated. These regular traits would ensure that the dog learns to avoid the situation of being groomed.

Although sometimes much easier with a puppy than with an older first timer, it is important that the dog learns that your hands on its body is a wonderful feeling. With most dogs just the sensation of touch is reward enough but some dogs have unfortunately learned that the human touch is not always as pleasant so for these dogs the process becomes a lot slower. We will first teach the dog that we are approachable and then move onto touching.

RECIPE 3

TOUCH ME

getting the dog used to handling

1. With the dog in the same room as you, click and toss the food treat to the dog. Repeat 3-4 times.

2. Raise the criteria by only clicking and treating when the dog looks at you. A confident dog will look to you for curiosity sake but even a wary dog will look at you but probably more because it wants to be aware of your next move.

3. Click and treat if the dog takes a step forward towards you. To achieve this, toss the food away from the dog towards the other side of the room, so that the dog must go past you in order to receive the reward.

4. Again raise the criteria; ensuring it is done in small increments, delay the click to ensure that the dog is closer to you each time. The behaviour the dog is learning is that it needs to be near you.

5. Once the dog is close to you withhold the click until the dog nudges you. Instead of tossing the food away from you, feed the dog from the hand furthest away from where the dog touched you. i.e. if the dog touched your hand or body from the left, feed from the right hand and vice versa.

6. Look for the dog using heavier or more forceful touches, or touches that last longer, i.e. click for the dog pushing into you.

7. As the dog seeks the contact, give contact back, with hands on different parts of their body. Step by step raise the criteria until the dog is receiving more and more handling, clicking each time you begin to touch the dog in a new place.

When touching the dog ensure your body posture is relaxed and that you do not become over-bearing by bending over the dog, which could instigate vulnerability fear from the dog. It may be necessary to crouch down beside the dog when attempting some of these exercises. If you keep your hand on the dog as you move to the different body parts, the dog will always know where your hand is and will be able to follow its progress, therefore try not to go directly to a new area of the dog.

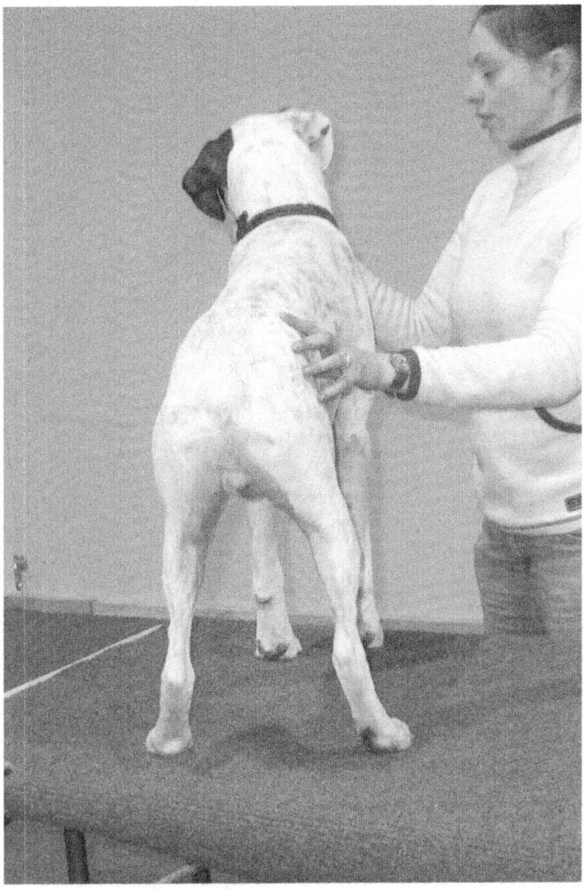

click the dog for pushing into your hand contact

touch different parts of the body, when the dog is in different positions

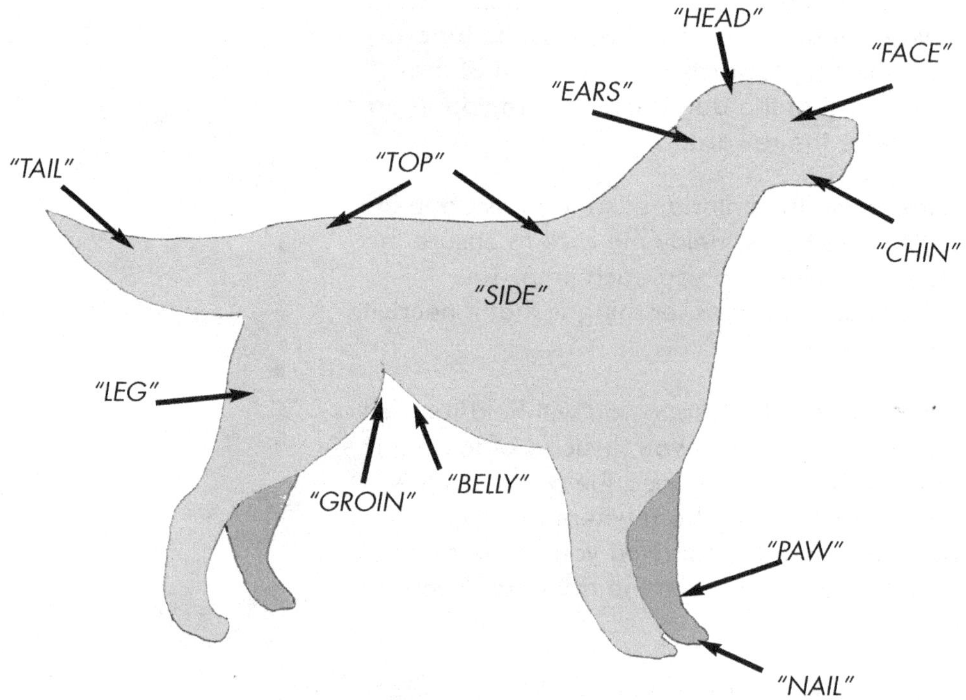

As you touch each area, name it as the dog will learn to associate that particular naming sound with the area on its body which will be helpful in the future. You may even want to name each foot individual, back-right-paw etc, but this would depend on how much training you wish to do, in the meantime generic terms are usually accepted by the dog.

Fingers tickling chin (Chin)

Hand stroking cheek (Face)

Hand resting on top of head (Head)

Hand moving around face and head, rubbing gently on ears (Ears)

Stroking neck and back (Top)

Running hand from neck, back and down each leg (Leg)

Then down the back and over the tail (Tail)

Lift the tail (Tail)

Then down each side of dog (Side)

Down the sides, underneath of the dog (Belly)

Down the insides of the legs (Leg)

Around the groin area (Groin)

Onto each paw without lifting it up (Paw)

Then lifting each paw (Paw)

Stroke each toe and nail (Nails)

8. The last step is to be able to touch each part of the dog without first running your hand down the other parts of the dog's body. It is a very confident dog that will allow this to happen which may take time with some dogs. By using the cues you can inform the dog of your intention, eventually the dog will offer you those parts of its body.

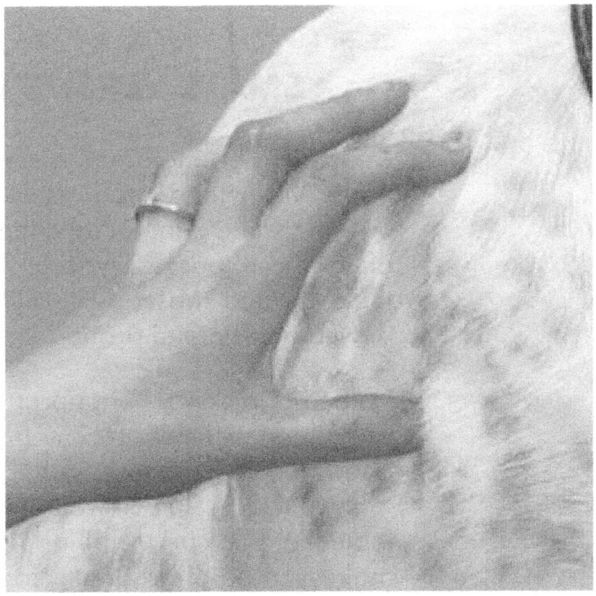

hand like a spider

RECIPE 4

REALLY, REALLY TOUCH ME

for dogs that are fearful of handling

If a dog has been carelessly handled, they can be fearful of approaching hands or any body language that may result in painful contact. We can teach these dog to pro-actively seek hand pressure.

1. Following on from Recipe 3 - Touch me, begin with the lightest, finger tip contact. Make your hand "like a spider" and rest your hand very lightly on the dogs shoulders, or any place they are confidently accepting contact.

2. Through your finger tips very slightly increase the weight of your hand, and click, when the dog pushes back into you. You will feel the muscles tense as the dog resists slightly - click this reaction. You will find it easier if someone else can hold the food pot, and feed the dog during this sensitive stage.

3. When the dog is able to react to contact with a confident push back, then begin to move your hands to different parts. Make a point of talking with your hands, so that the dog knows where your hands are travelling, and when to push back.

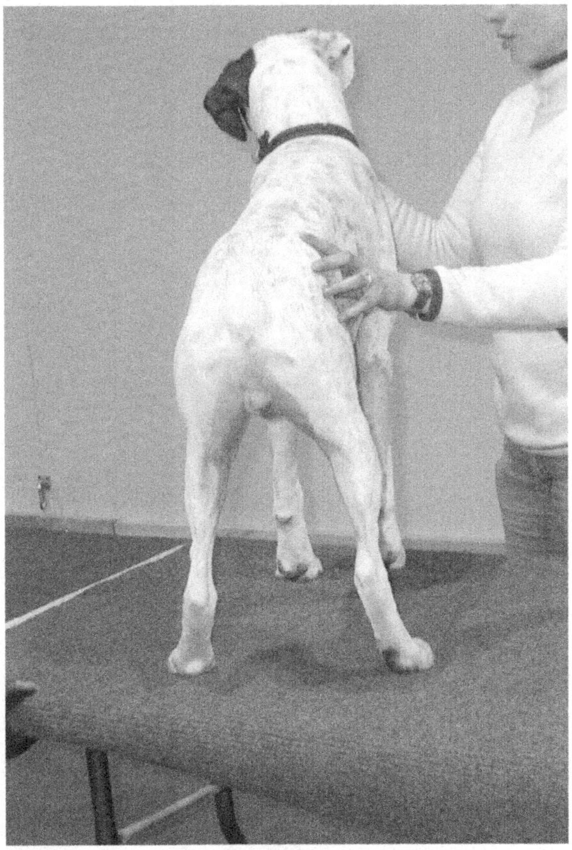

pushing back against contact

By teaching a physically sensitive dog to work into the pressure, they forget about avoiding contact. The subsequent reinforcement for this action makes the whole process become enjoyable.

SMALL VERSUS LARGE DOGS

Depending on the breed a small dog can take as long or even longer than some large dogs, the methods work as well with any size dog as effectively all dogs are hardwired with the same general thinking and behaviour patterns. However small dogs are often afflicted with our ability to be able to more easily physically manipulate them, due to their size and subsequently lighter weight. For a similar reason, large dogs are often moved and hauled around in an unfashionable process.

Instead of picking them up and moving them around to whatever position or place we want them, consider teaching your dog to jump and climb onto an object on cue. If the dog is too large then targeting them onto a towel or mat on the floor should be enough to keep them in place while grooming. If the dog is able and if you have a bench or table that you can use, then having the dog up on a surface at about our waist height makes the art of grooming for us much more comfortable. It also means it gives the dog less inclination to move away during the process. The difference between jumping and climbing is that climbing gives the dog more control of his body, and is generally a steadier and quieter process. Not all dogs are physically able to jump or may lack the confidence but at the same time will quite happily climb or walk over an object.

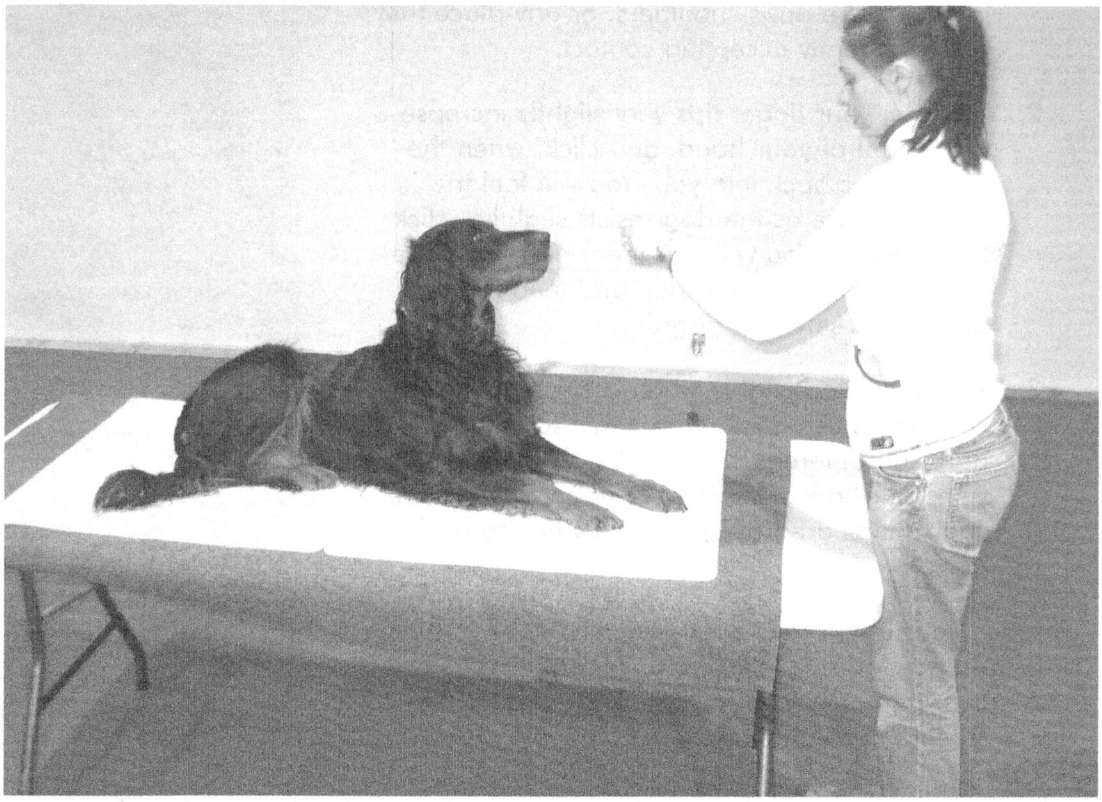

grooming on a table top - with a non slip surface and the dog's target mat

RECIPE 5

TEACHING YOUR DOG TO CLIMB

Most dogs will naturally jump up onto a surface or find the quickest way into something, like your car etc. Physical momentum propels them more easily and uses muscle power quickly and efficiently. However there may be times when you need your dog to take more time and be more aware of where they are stepping or what they are getting onto. For instance if you want to use a nice table, bench or dresser in order to have your dog stand for grooming, you certainly don't want the dog to scratch the surface with its nails as it tries to come to a skidding halt. Teaching your dog to climb, both up and down onto a surface helps the dog learn to be aware of and control its body on a more specific basis and can also help them to learn to slow their movements. Dogs love routines and love using those set routines to anticipate what is going to happen next, but for some dogs the act of anticipation itself can make them rush headlong into something without due care, which of course can not only be dangerous for their health but can also cause unnecessary stress if something gets broken in the process.

In order to get your dog to climb you will need to create some form of stepping system. Consider using chairs, low boxes, thick sturdy books (telephone books can be ideal) or even if you have them, use a low two or three rung stepladder or a ramp. Placement of the objects near a wall can also be important to ensure that the dog feels secure when working the equipment. Whatever you use always ensure that the surface is not slippery - this can be achieved by using a damp towel, carpet or rubber matting.

CLIMB UP

As a trainer you have to be able to mark the movements more precisely to ensure that the dog does not start to gather its body in readiness for leaping.

1. Placing the first step in front of the dog, click for any behaviour where the dog is heading towards the step.

2. For the first few times throw the reward away from the step to encourage movement towards it, but as you don't want to teach the dog to climb with speed limit this to 3-4 repetitions.

3. Withhold the click until the dog makes an effort to touch the step with a foot, click when effort is made. Take the reward to the dog.

   If you click for a nose touch the dog will not be able to make its body go past holding the step with its nose and therefore progress will be very limited. By taking the reward to the dog you can perform two actions, one of keeping the dog in place on that first step, and the other of lifting the dog's head up so that its nose doesn't hold onto the step (if you have a strong nose touching dog).

4. When the behaviour of keeping that foot on the first step is consistent then withhold the click until you get the next foot on the first step.

   Clicking for the same foot moving to the next step causes the dog's muscles to move into a position that will encourage jumping, which is the movement we are trying to avoid.

5. Your next movement is determined with both front feet on the first step and whether you will need either both front feet on the next step or one of the back feet to come up to the first step. This is dependent on how long and how deep you have made your steps in relation to your dog's size.

   If using a low short stepping system then getting the front feet on the next step is probably best as the whole dog may not fit on the first step, but if your system is high, i.e. climbing onto a chair then the dog will need to bring its back feet up before being able to go further.

6. Once the dog is in such a position that the next step will be moving its back feet onto the first step. Click as soon as one of the back legs is lifted, or as soon as you see weight shifting from one of the back feet as this indicates next movement.

   This is dependent on how much behaviour your dog offers in any session, some dogs can handle offering a lot of action before being clicked while other dogs need smaller increments in order to know that they are on the right path to reward. Although I do believe that some dogs learn to offer only a little so that they can get rewarded more often - sometimes you wonder who the trainer is and who is being trained!

7. Repeat until you are sure that the lifting of the back leg is the action being clicked.

   Remember to keep hand delivering the food so that the dog maintains the position. If your dog has not learned how to take food gently, then placing the food within reach on the steps can also be a way of maintaining position. However we don't really want the dog just looking for food on its way up the climb.

8. Work the back foot up so that the dog makes an effort to step onto the step with its back foot and also put weight on it. Click for any movement forward or up, but ensure that the dog's movement is deliberate, not speedy.

   It is often this step that is the hardest to get the dog to perform; perhaps this is where the last effort of commitment to the journey is made and therefore removes the feeling of security.

9. With three feet on various stages of the steps the dog needs to be encouraged to move forward. It is the front movement that is again the focus point. Repeat the above parts of the recipe but where the first step is the beginning.

   Luring can be an effective way to encourage the dog to move forward, but the focus that we really want is for the dog to concentrate on its body parts rather than focusing on the reward alone.

Building confidence to choose to be on the table top, but letting the dog teach itself, not luring.

CLIMB DOWN

Most dogs will happily jump down from a reasonable height but to do so can cause them injury if they are not athletic or are smaller than they think they are. A friend's Pomeranian leapt from her arms onto their carpeted floor and broke a front leg, and she did it twice in one year!

As a dog jumps it pushes off with its back legs and depending on the surface from which it is leaping it may knock a stifle or foot on the journey, let alone misjudge the distance - all of these things can scare a dog off repeating the behaviour or associating it with the table. It becomes just as important to teach the dog to climb down steps where possible.

To teach the dog to climb down is exactly the same as teaching them to climb up but the trick is in slowing them down enough to take the steps properly.

1. Work on clicking for small movements rather than looking for the end result.
2. Click as the dog is working its way down not once it is off the steps at the bottom. If the dog thinks that being at the bottom of the steps is the required behaviour it will try to get there as fast as possible, causing it to jump.

NERVOUS DOGS

Even dogs that have learned to dislike the grooming process can with patience learn to tolerate or even revel in being spruced up. I have seen dogs both semi and fully sedated in readiness for grooming because they have unfortunately learned that grooming is a painful, scary process and if not sedated will wind themselves up so much that not only do they really stress out but everyone, groomer and owner alike will stress too.

It is not pleasant to try and groom a dog that is yelping, yelling, nipping, panting, fidgeting and generally challenging everything that comes near it. And it certainly isn't pleasant for an owner to see their beloved pet get itself into any type of frenzy. It is an unfortunate reality that sometimes our fears and superstitions are translated to the dog. Throughout all my years I have always heard (and still do) people threaten and tease their dog with a bath or a haircut like it is some form of punishment, so it is not surprising that dogs learn that it is a process that is to be avoided at all costs. But given the opportunity to create the right calm circumstances I have also seen those once sedated dogs learn to tolerate if not actually enjoy being groomed.

The pure relief for all concerned, dog, groomer and owner is obvious, especially when those same dogs eventually come running to meet you for a groom, or no longer have to be dragged into the grooming salon. I have also seen other dogs go from being very mouthy and snappy to learning how to settle down and stop screeching or snapping at any anticipated tug of hair. Some of the best responses come when a dog is so relaxed that they actually take the time to snooze whilst being groomed - of course this doesn't always help when you need them to stand or turn around but I'd rather the dog was totally comfortable and trusting.

OLDER OR PHYSICALLY CHALLENGED DOGS

As the dog gets older it can become more difficult for them to move around with the same agility of their younger years, and it can also be uncomfortable for them to remain in one position, especially standing, for any length of time. Older dog's skin and hair can become thinner and therefore they feel the groom more sensitively. It is important that the dog's physical needs are catered for, and especially so when they get older. Often they can no longer offer the appropriate behaviours for an easy groom so in order to continue keeping their trust we must learn to manipulate them comfortably and reward them for what they can offer us.

Even dogs that have lost or are losing their hearing or sight can still be clicker trained, or at least the methods can be used. The cue becomes a touch in a certain area and the reward can still be given for the appropriate movement. Old dogs that have never particularly enjoyed being groomed can learn to trust and begin to appreciate the comfort that a respectful and caring groom can give.

Older dogs seem to especially appreciate being groomed; the invigoration from the groom gives them a renewed vitality for a few days and from reports given by owners even for a few weeks. Sometimes older dogs seem to inherit a particular doggy odour associated with age that may be distressing to the owner, so bathing them on a more regular basis becomes important. They also tend to have more focus on comfort and especially are more focused on food than some of their younger counterparts, so they can still be easily motivated.

I have seen a lot of owners not bath or groom their elderly dogs because they believe that the dog will hate the process and they do not want to see their dog suffer. What is often not seen is the care and respectfulness that goes into bathing an elderly or physically challenged dog and the resulting rejuvenation that the dog obviously feels. Owners often tell me that their older dog acts like a puppy again for a few days after a good bath and groom. And the extra amount of attention that is given to an older dog, with pats, cuddles and comments can only make for the dog to feel like a star.

CATS

Cats need to be groomed too, mostly they perform this function themselves but occasionally they will need help. Cats are being bred with more and more hair and are just as likely to moult as dogs are. The methods outlined in this book can easily be applied to a cat, and are much preferable to use, as cats are quick to scratch and bite anyone that gives them grief.

A couple of notes if you are going to use these methods for your cat:

- Keep the treats small.

- Train more often rather than for prolonged periods.
- Be careful about using temperature, as cats tend to be more sensitive to heat changes.
- If you are going to dry your cat with a hair-dryer, the small hand held one is better as the forceful dryer will probably be too scary.

3 Bath Time

BATHING

Generally when we decide to give our dogs a bath its because we feel that they really need it and that unless they have a bath they will not be allowed back in the house, or its because we don't want to touch them, and then we mentally prepare ourselves in readiness for resistance - the dog of course maybe oblivious to what's actually going to happen but they are not oblivious to the tension that their owner is beginning to display.

If we believe it's going to be a battle before we even start then the dog will sense this and everyone prepares for the war that's about to happen. Even if the dog does desperately need a bath and has never had one, by delaying the bath for even a short while and instead training the dog to go into the bathing area can prevent war from breaking out for every future bath.

Giving the dog a bath often follows this procedure:

- Get many towels from cupboard
- Get dog's shampoo from cupboard - for some reason we often don't keep their shampoo anywhere near our own!
- Run the bath/shower
- Call dog to us
- Go find dog
- Drag dog out from under the dining room table
- Take dog by collar to bathing area
- Physically lift or push dog into bath/shower
- Wet dog, shampoo, lather and rinse - all while trying to hold dog in place
- Try to get towel around dog before it jumps out of bath
- Hold another towel up to try and stop getting wet from dog shaking excess water off
- Yell at other family members to open up all doorways to the outside (because we forgot to do this earlier) so that dog can take a direct route to the outside

- Run after dog, chasing it outside because it keeps shaking excess water off in every room it passes through
- Try to towel dry dog once it is outside and prevent the dog from coming back inside until it is fairly dry
- Clean up bathroom and vow that someone else in the family will wash the dog next time!

So let's imagine another possible scenario:

- Get many towels from cupboard
- Get dog's shampoo from cupboard - same reason as before as to why we often don't keep their shampoo anywhere near our own!
- Run the bath/shower
- No need to call dog to us as dog is already with us of his/her own free will
- Dog hops into the bath/shower when asked
- Wet dog, shampoo, lather and rinse - all while dog waits or turns as requested
- Get towel around dog while it waits patiently in the bath
- Use a few towels to vigorously rub dog all over to get most of the excess moisture off
- Ask dog to hop out of bath onto bath mat while you finish towel drying him/her
- Give the dog a treat as you tell him that he doesn't need to be in the bathing area anymore
- Pick up wet towels and take to laundry!

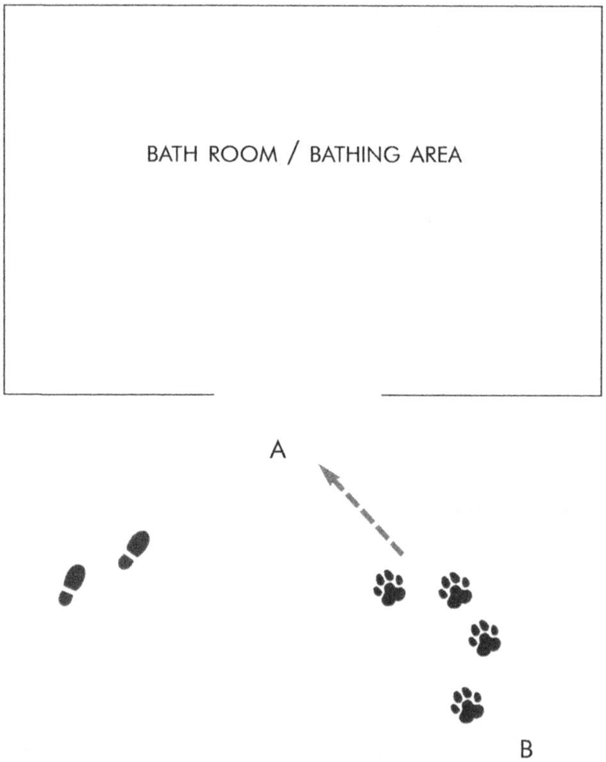

RECIPE 6

INTO THE BATHING AREA

Although we could teach the dog just to go into the bathing apparatus, some dogs are nervous of being anywhere near the area that holds the bath, so in order to overcome that fear first you may need to retrain the dog that the bathing area is actually a good place to be.

1. With both you and your dog standing outside the bathing area and the entrance to the bathing area between you, throw a piece of food so that it lands just outside the entrance to the bathing room (A), click when the dog takes a step towards the food (effectively towards the bathing room entrance).

   If the dog does not actually take a step, then you or the dog may need to start further away from the entrance to encourage more forward movement. This is effectively luring the dog to perform the behaviour of walking towards the bathing area. Repeat 2-3 times.

   Be careful to lure no more than 3 times.

2. Patiently wait for the repetition of the forward movement that you got from luring. Click for forward movement.

   By throwing the reward so that it lands behind and past the dog (B), the dog will turn around to get the reward but then turn back and take more steps forward to come back towards you.

3. Increase the criteria by clicking for more movement and more specifically movement towards the bathing room entrance.

going for a bath - off lead, and by choice

By turning your body to face the entrance you can give the dog a clue as to where you want them to go. Ensure you raise the criteria quickly so as not to allow the dog to think the behaviour remains outside the bathing room entrance.

4. Again withhold the click and wait for the dog to take a step into the bathing area.

   Remember you are still outside, so the dog should be taking a step in, being clicked and then receiving the reward outside the area (C) - this way the dog is getting much repetition in walking towards and into the bathing area. You should find that once the dog is confident of the behaviour it would start heading towards the bathing area at a faster pace.

If you tried to start this exercise where you were positioned in the bathing area and the dog was outside, so that you were trying to lure the dog in, the process would slow down. The dog will see you as the reason for going into the bathing area and because the reward point would be outside the door the behaviour the dog would learn first would be just to look at you, not that forward movement into the area is the behaviour required.

5. Continue to raise the criteria until the dog is going further into the bathing area and both happily and speedily.

The environment will be the cue for this behaviour. Just as the dog is aware it was somewhere associated with anxiety, they will soon associate it with rewards and pleasure.

Alternatively use a target mat inside the bathing area that the dog can go to. Teach the targeting outside and away from the bathing area and gradually move it towards and into the area. The idea is that the targeting behaviour overcomes the fear of the environment. Depending on how nervous the dog is will govern how quickly or slowly you proceed.

You will need to ensure that you reduce the target mat so that the dog is confident to enter the bathing area without the target mat in place.

RECIPE 7

BATH TIME

Depending on the size of the dog and the placement of the apparatus that you are bathing the dog in will depend on how you work the dog to getting into the bathing equipment.

Remember with small dogs you may need to create steps for them to go up, telephone books or low boxes onto a chair next to the bath may help. You may need to also give them a way down into the bath. With older or physically impaired dogs you will probably need to create something that gives both you and the dog support should you need to lift the dog into the bath.

Have everything ready to go before you start training, you don't necessarily have to set it all up as this can be done while training the dog - use the interruptions to keep the dog interested in what is happening and it also gives both you and the dog a quick mental break.

1. Position yourself in the bathing room and click/treat the dog a few times for coming in and out of the bath area as before.

   Ensure you throw the food out of the room so that you know the dog knows that the behaviour is to enter the room.

2. Raise the criteria of the dog heading towards the bathing equipment, only clicking for movement towards it.

   Even looks towards the equipment may get an initial click so that the dog is focusing on that rather than you.

   If you position yourself mid-way between the door and the bath (depending of course on the size of your bathing area), ensure you face your body mainly towards the bath. Dogs will often come around to look at your face in order to try and read what it is that you want. This is one way of encouraging the dog to step closer to the apparatus, but be careful not to make the looking at you the behaviour that you are training.

This would also be another good opportunity to use a target mat, but the use of a non-slip mat or towel in the bath or shower can also offer a clue to the dog - dogs are naturally curious so will often check out new things in their environment.

The use of some form of non-slip surface is extremely important here as the dog needs to gain confidence when getting in and out of the bath, and a simple slip either on entry or exit could set the training back.

For dogs that are already extremely anxious about the bath, begin by teaching the dog to jump in and out of a box to gain confidence. You can use the target mat in the box to transfer the final behaviour to the actual bath. (*opposite page*).

3. Work the dog up to the bath and then raise the criteria so that the dog makes an effort to lift its paw or rest its head on the edge of the bath, for shower boxes the dog may go to lift its leg to step on the edge of the box.

Building confidence

Left: dog climbs in but gets reward thrown outside

Below: reinforcement for standing in box

Right: sitting and turning - exercises to build confidence

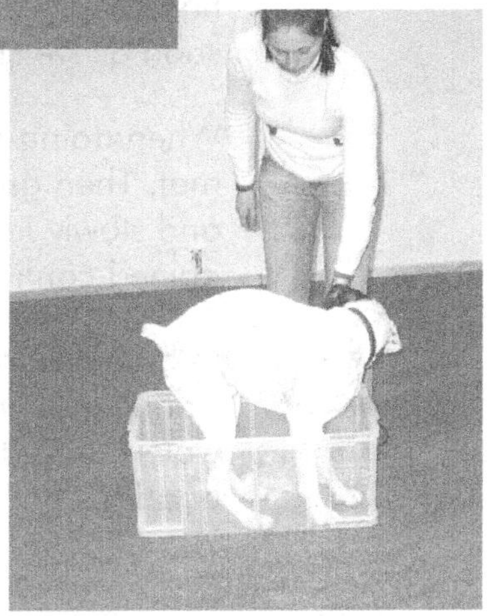

4. Keep raising the criteria so that the dog continues to make more effort but ensure that they are getting enough feedback (click/treating) to encourage them to continue working.

5. Once the dog is standing on the edge of the bath, start rewarding them in position and clicking them for looking into the bath.

6. Raise the criteria so that the dog starts to try and get in the bath.

7. Finally withhold the click until the dog makes a real effort to get in.

8. You now need to also click and treat the exit from the bath. The dog will naturally exit the bath of its own accord, if not encourage your dog to exit the bath in the same manner it got in by tossing a piece of food or a toy outside of the bath. Click as the dog exits the bath and throw the food back into the bath.

The dog should be confident enough to get back into the bath to retrieve the food, when it does start adding a cue like "In Bath" just as the dog gets in. Add a cue just before your dog naturally gets out of the bath and then click and treat.

It's a good idea to take this opportunity to ensure that your "Wait" cue is also generalised to remaining in the bath until invited out with an "Out" cue.

Even though the running of the bath and the getting of special shampoos and towels will cue the dog that it is bath-time, it is better for you if your dog only gets into the bath when invited to do so!

I trained Vienna at my parent's house as their bath is not very deep. However next time the dogs went to stay my mother informed me that Vienna spent much of her weekend getting the bath-pillow out of the bath! It became so ingrained in her from the one session that we did that even months later when renting a weekend holiday house, the first thing Vienna did when we made a tour of the property was to jump in the bath as soon as we stepped into the bathroom. Thus the importance of cueing behaviours!

When doing this for the first few times, ensure there is no water in the bath, only the bath mat. Then gradually raise the criteria by adding water, first to a minimal puddle level and slowly increasing the level. However by this time you may find that your dog has gained confidence regardless of the water level.

In bathing dogs both at home and for work I have found that dogs do not actually like standing in water and that they much prefer a shower type system or to at least have the water poured quietly over them. I usually start from the feet upwards and leave the head and face until last.

Important tips to remember when bathing the dog:

- try not to get water in the dog's ears - use cotton wool to plug the ear if you are concerned that you might.
- The face needs to be cleaned. Better to lather your hands and rub gently over the face, avoiding getting soap-suds in the dogs ears, nose or mouth.
- If the dog's head is tilted downwards during rinsing the water will not get into their eyes, ears, nose and mouth. Check out the recipe 13 (page 47) for head tilting if your dog doesn't already do this.

Often we are happy with just having the dog get into the bath and stay there. Some dogs we can easily bend over to get to all body parts. If your dog is small and hard to reach, think about getting the dog to climb onto something in the bath to make your job easier and less strain on your back.

The idea behind training your dog in grooming is to allow them to work for the reward of having you groom them; plus if we find the task pleasant we are also more likely to repeat the process - no point in us suffering either!

BODY CUES

The dog's first language is that of the body, its movements, posture and positions. We can use our own body movements to cue the dog for specific behaviours such as turning, coming, moving away or even as a target. Out of a natural curiosity dogs will often face the same direction that we face, however having a dog face the opposite way is a necessity of grooming.

TURNING THE DOG AROUND IN THE BATH

Teaching the dog to turn on cue and perhaps even target an article at one end of the bath will help you to bathe both sides of the dog effectively. Teach the following away from the bath and then generalise the behaviour before attempting it with the dog in the bath. Instead of using your hand for a touch target, try using a target mat for the dog to go to or allow the dog to follow a target stick. General grooming accessories can be used to target the dog, try using a brush or a towel to direct the dog, or you could even use bath toys if you want to. The other great aspect about using targets though is they will help teach the dog to hold a position.

RECIPE 8

TURN

1. Place a reward in your palm and then hold in place with your thumb, position your hand sideways in front of dog and click as the dog moves forward to investigate the food, release the reward to dog. Repeat this a couple of times.

2. Repeat the above action but do not release the lure, instead reward the dog from the hand opposite to the one that holds the lure. Ideally the dog will touch one hand and then turn to take the reward from the other hand.

3. Remove the reward lure in your touch hand but maintain the same position, click for touching the hand and again reward from the non-touch hand. You have now changed the "bribe" into a "reward".

4. By using your hands you are asking the dog to touch one hand and then turn to get the reward from the other hand, the dog is then turning of its own free will without being cued. What you have taught is a targeting behaviour, the next step is to change that to a different cue and fade out the target.

5. Once the dog is confidently turning to touch a hand, add a cue "turn" just before the dog turns.

6. Slowly begin to fade out the holding up of the hand (body cue) while repeating the cue "turn", always ensure the dog maintains at least the minimum action before clicking.

The next important part to bathing the dog is getting them to wait before being released from the bath. I always find it useful to get as much excess water from the dog's coat as possible before releasing them from the bath.

DRYING

Many dogs are dried with a quick vigorous rub with half a dozen towels or more and then directed to the outside, hopefully by the shortest and quickest route through the house. The dog is then left outside to fully dry off, which for some dogs may only be a few minutes while for others it takes hours, all dependent on the volume and density of their coat and how the weather is.

Thoroughly drying the dog after a bath (or even after it has been swimming or out in the rain) can help prevent matted hair forming, make it easier to de-tangle knots and trim the dog, which generally keeps them in a comfortable and healthy manner.

It depends on the breed of dog you have as to how much you invest in drying equipment, but generally everyone has a towel or two spare that they keep just for drying the dog. The use of a hair dryer can significantly decrease drying time, the following recipes will show you how to introduce it along with a few notes on good practices to make drying that much easier.

Interestingly enough the drier the dog becomes after being wet, the less likely it is to run around the house, rubbing itself on furniture and the carpet, or even outside where they have that tendency to roll around on the grass or anything else that they believe will help them get dry. This sometimes negatives the point of giving them a bath!

TOWELS

I've yet to meet a dog that hasn't loved being rubbed down all over with a towel. The positive reinforcement that they get from being touched all over must feel very invigorating. So, it's always a good idea to have a few towels on hand so that you can dry the dog as much as possible before it is ready to run around the house.

When Connor was young I made such fun out of towel drying him, especially while holding onto him in order to rub him all over with the towel, that whenever he gets wet he runs up to people in order to dry himself off. Doesn't matter who it is or even whether they have bare legs or not, he will make a direct line for a person and proceed to rub up against them - my friends are often warned but often it's only once have they been dried on do they do the "Connor's wet dance". I must say he is very subtle though as he slides up against you, you would think he's just being friendly!

The hardest thing about drying the dog with a towel is trying to get the dog as dry as possible before they get out of the bath. Having bathed many dogs I have tried to use the towel as a cue that it is now ok for the dog to shake. The cue comes at the point where I hold the towel up really to shield me from getting wet from the spray of water. It is natural for the dog to want to shake during the bathing process, cueing them to wait or stand and touching them on either their rump or their shoulders seems to prevent a full shake which can help you not to get as wet too.

SMALL HAIR DRYER

A small hand-held hair dryer (as we use for ourselves) can gently and slowly dry the dog with hot, warm or cold air while being used all over the body. Temperature control is needed to ensure the dog is not burned or chilled, and temperature also affects hair volume, the hotter the temperature the more body and frizzy the hair is given.

Getting a dog to accept the noise and the fan of the dryer is important. I regularly wash a Jack Russell Terrier called Churchill that used to bark continually while the dryer was on, with a pronounced effort of biting at it when it faced or was lifted towards him. By introducing the click and treat system Churchill has now accepted the dryer and the barking has been drastically reduced and the biting at it is now non-existent.

RECIPE 9

GETTING USED TO THE HAIR DRYER

Start with the hair dryer off and click at each stage to reinforce the dryer as a positive:

1. Put the dryer on table next to dog and let dog look at, sniff or investigate it. It's ok if the dog ignores it.

2. Pick the dryer up and move it from hand to hand.

3. Then move it in your hand around the dog.

4. Place the dryer back on the table facing it away from the dog.
5. Turn the dryer on to the lowest fan setting and leave on the table.
6. Turn the hair dryer over so that it is now facing the dog but is still on the table.

Only dogs that are really comfortable with the dryer and its function should (and only if really necessary) ever have the dryer pointed towards their head and face.

At all times you should be clicking and rewarding and maintaining a casual non-fussy approach to the training.

Now you should be ready to use the dryer on the dog.

7. Lift the dryer up and let the air blow on the dog, start with the back top part of the dog (rump).
8. Slowly bring the dryer up, around and over the dog's body, being careful not to blow the dryer in the dog's face.
9. Before changing the setting to full fan place the dryer back on the bench facing away from the dog and then repeat the above process.

I have noticed that most dogs are quite comfortable with a dryer being used on them as long as it is introduced in a positive and non-threatening manner. I will often start using the dryer while still rubbing the dog with a towel. Most dogs will check the noise and the fan but in a comfortable secure environment will readily accept its use.

HIGH POWERED DRYER

Most professionals will also use a high-powered dryer specifically designed for pushing the water out of the coat quickly as it vigorously pushes the moisture from the coat, which is brilliant for removing excess undercoat and dead hair. Certainly if you have multiple dogs and ones with heavy shedding coats this type of dryer is very worthwhile.

These types of dryers can be quite noisy and push air from them at a high rate so extra special care needs to be taken in introducing its use to the dog. I have actually found that the older dogs especially, learn to love the high-powered dryer because it can massage their skin with a similar force that scratching themselves with their hind legs has, and as the dog gets older their own force or ability to do this is diminished.

It may not be wise to use such a forceful dryer on very small dogs, but it would depend on the dog's robustness and the need. Small dogs don't often have the excess coat that benefits from this type of water removal - one towel will generally remove as much as the force dryer. However if the dog is well generalised to noise and sensation then using this dryer will still help dry and fluff their coat well.

RECIPE 10

GETTING USED TO THE HIGH POWERED DRYER

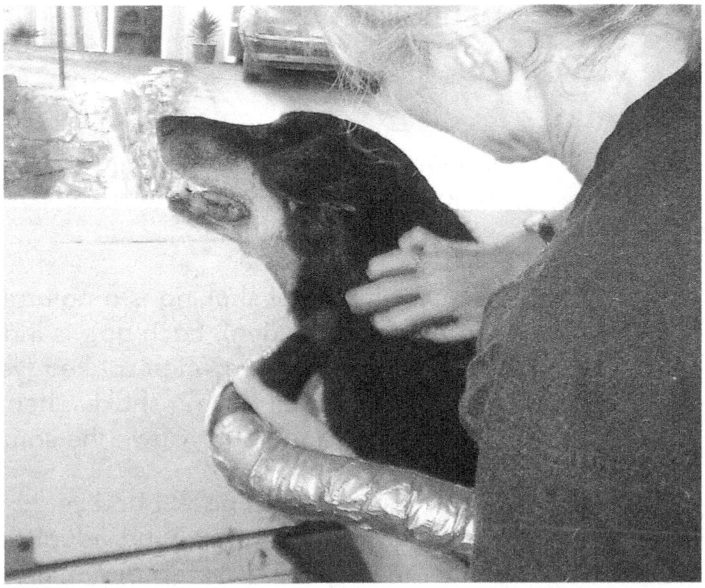

enjoying the high power dryer

Again start with the hair dryer off and click at each stage to reinforce the dryer as a positive. I would also recommend having the power part of the dryer away from the dog, as this is the noisiest part:

1. As you will need to hold the dryer, show the dog what it is and let dog look at, sniff or investigate it. Again it does not matter if the dog isn't really interested - after all it is only a piece of plastic.

   These types of dryers should **NEVER** be pointed towards a dog's head or face. They are far too powerful and could easily cause damage.

2. With the nozzle pointing well away from the dog, turn the dryer on, firstly on the lowest setting then once the dog is happy with the dryer gradually increase the settings.

   Maintaining the dog in a touch or target position will help give it the trust of you that is needed during this time.

3. Lift the dryer up and as you bring it around to face the dog hold it perpendicular to the dog's back so that the air just skims over the top of their back, then gently lower it so that the dryer air is connecting with the dog.

4. Move back and forth over the dog's back and then move down the dog's sides, front and rear.

Always ensure the nozzle is pointing down or away from the dog's face. Some dogs will accept the dryer all over their body while others do not like it near the front of their bodies.

Whenever you use a dryer, respect the dog's feelings; don't misuse the trust that you are building up with them. After time the dog may come to accept something that can be as scary as the high-powered dryer, the clicker makes it easy but as a trainer we must remember that some dogs may take longer to actually enjoy some of the behaviours that we ask of them.

RECIPE 11

SHAKE

To teach a dog to shake on cue can be very handy as it means you can control when the majority of excess water can be removed, let alone be prepared so that you don't get so wet while bathing the dog.

Because the act of shaking is a natural behaviour for a dog, to capture it using the clicker would be ideal. Each dog is individual in when it shakes. I have groomed dogs that continually shake when soaked (yep, I get wet), and those that don't ever shake even when soaked, that have a shake when the water touches their neck and wither areas or even when a light touch down the same area occurs.

At the writing of this book I had yet to work out a method that would work on every dog so I believe it is best if the individual dog is assessed for when it has a shake and the trainer then set up the scenario to either capture the behaviour or elicit a shake from the dog. I would also repeat a cue of "Shake" whenever the dog was doing this, and reward the dog accordingly - if you happen to be close to the dog when it shakes and you get wet - remember to either wear waterproof clothing or learn to move fast!

Some dogs will shake after waking and stretching so its not only water that will make them offer this behaviour.

Good luck with this one and if you figure out a sure fire method that will work with the majority of dogs I would love to hear from you. When we set up for the photos for this book we actually worked out a way to get Connor to shake, we asked him to stand still and gently poured a small bucket of water over him, he did a shake every time (it's not a method I would recommend unless your dog is very willing) - and he came back willingly to repeat the performance about a dozen times. This is a perfect example of the trust that can occur between dog and owner if the clicker and positive methods are used for all training.

4 Cueing Movements

A dog is a biological being that feels pain and will move itself to attain more comfort during a prolonged process. As grooming can be fairly prolonged it is helpful if the dog is able to perform more than the basics in order to ease the process. The following recipes are also helpful in manipulating the dog into different positions and poses to allow for easy brushing, combing and clipping.

HEAD MOVEMENTS

Teaching the dog to tilt or turn their head on cue can help in many situations during the grooming process. Often we need the dog to hold its head up high, look downwards or even look left or right. It gives us the ability to look at the dog from different angles while up close and personal, and it means that the dog has moved body parts out of the way so that we can access other parts more readily.

Some examples of where head movements can help:

- Clipping under the chin and down the neck.
- The hairs on the ears of many breeds need combing out, clipping, trimming or thinning.
- Checking for evenness in facial hair.
- Looking downwards stretches the head to neck skin for evenness of clipping.

I do wonder sometimes whether some breeds have an inbuilt sensor that works a certain way depending on what body part is being groomed. Many a poodle will try to cover its front leg with its head in order to hide the appendage that you are trying to brush.

RECIPE 12

HEAD UP/LOOK UP

1. With the dog sitting (or standing) in front, lure the dog to look up. Click for any head lifting or upward movement, regardless of how small. Even the dog's eyes moving upwards can be clicked.

   Be careful to click only for the head movement and not the shoulders lifting, we need the dog to move its head up but keep its feet planted firmly on the floor.

2. Ensure you give the reward in the opposite direction to the way you want your dog to look. The act of the dog bringing its head back up is part of the process to click. Repeat a couple of times.

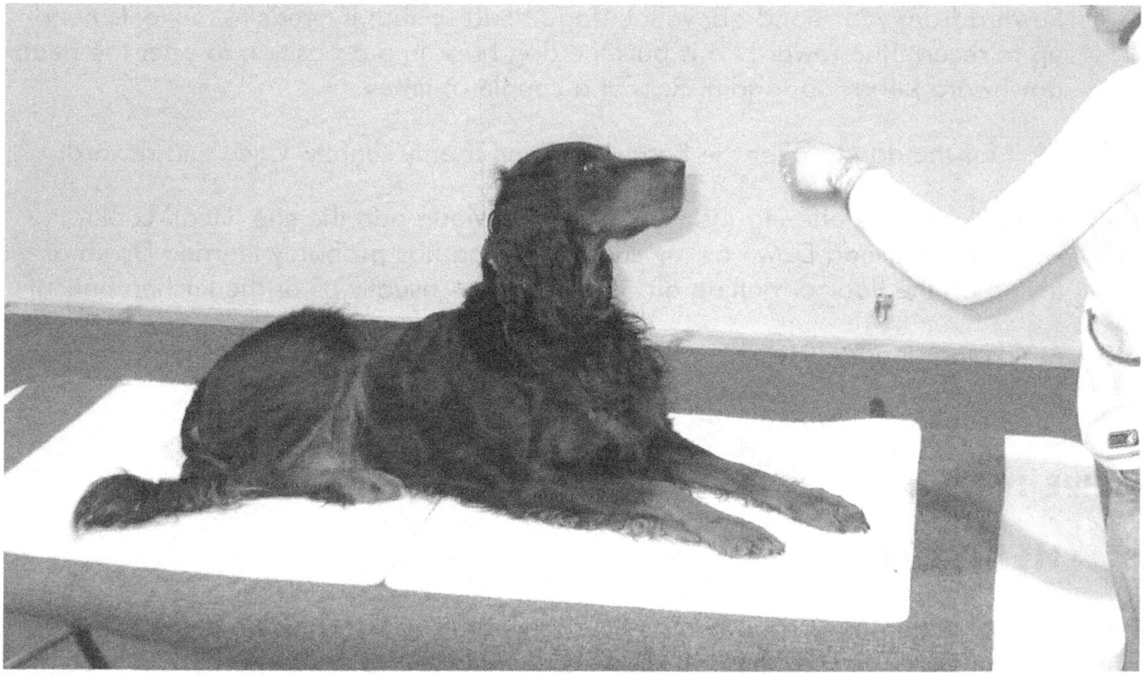

3. Instead of luring wait for the dog to offer the behaviour even if only slightly. Click and reward.

4. Continue to mark the behaviour until you can accurately tell when the dog is about to offer it.

5. Once the dog is offering the consistent behaviour, add the cue "Head Up", I would refrain from using "Up" as this cue is often used in other parts of life.

6. Ensure you proof the behaviour to only occur during training when it is cued.

RECIPE 13

HEAD DOWN/LOOK DOWN

1. Ideally you would teach this by having the dog sit in front of you and capture any head movement downward. However luring is quite acceptable. Using a reward in your hand move it downward a small distance from your dog. Click when the head moves downward.

   If you do not want to use food, try tapping the floor with your foot to encourage the dog to look towards the sound.

2. Reward from your hand above the dog's head so that it needs to move its head up to receive the reward. This puts the dog back into a position to offer the head downward behaviour again. Repeat a couple of times
3. Wait for the dog to offer the behaviour even if only slightly. Click and reward.
4. Once the dog is offering the consistent behaviour, add the cue "Head Look". I wouldn't use Head Down as my cue as the dog has probably learned Down as laying on the floor or getting off of something - usually us or the kitchen bench!
5. Maintain a longer "Head Look" cue by withholding the click for gradual increases in time and using your Wait and Ok for release cues.

RECIPE 14

HEAD ON

This is where the dog purposely rests its head on whatever is closest to it. You could hold your hand out, palm up and the dog rests his head in your palm or perhaps if grooming close to the couch, the dog could rest his head on the arm of the chair. For a Gordon Setter this is a very natural behaviour, many a Gordon has a heavy head and they quickly learn how to rest it on a variety of objects including human body parts - and they are not fussy as to which ones either! I taught Connor to fetch a cushion, lie down with the cushion between his front feet and place his head on the cushion - a very cute party trick! However it also worked well when I was re-teaching agility contacts where I needed him to dip his head as the end behaviour. It's always our own imagination that holds us back as to what is possible in teaching and generalising those behaviours that we have taught our dogs.

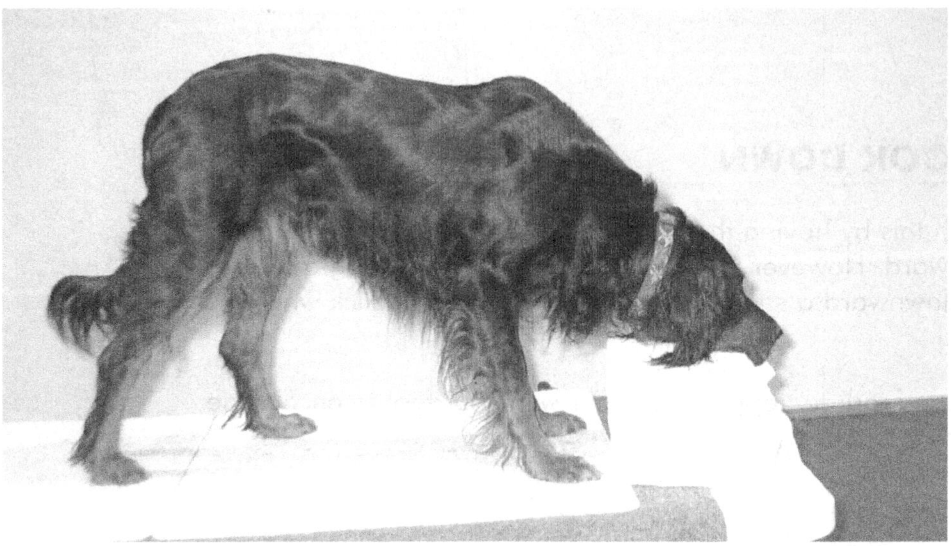

"Head on" the chin resting on a box. The position can be used for standing or lying down.

In grooming this is a good way of getting the dog to keep its head still while you are using scissors or combs and brushes around the face, especially around the eyes and mouth. One quick move could be disastrous. Interestingly enough with grooming practice one becomes very adapt at moving quickly with the dog in order to avoid such disasters - and many an intake of breath I have heard from onlookers when grooming around the eyes when the dog does move.

1. Teach this by having something underneath the chin that the dog could touch as it lowers its head. Alternatively touching the dog underneath the chin with a flat hand (palm facing down) and clicking at the same time as the touch can easily teach the dog what behaviour is required.

2. Touch your hand or the object gently to the dog's chin and click as it touches. Repeat a few times.

3. With the object just underneath the dog's chin, but not touching wait for the dog to do a chin touch on the object. Click and reward.

The object acts like a target, when the dog sees the object it will be natural to push his chin onto it.

4. Once the dog is offering the consistent behaviour, add the cue "Head On"

5. Maintain a longer Head On cue by withholding the click for gradual increases in time and using your Wait and Ok for release cues.

RECIPE 15

HEAD LEFT

In a similar fashion to the Head On cue, teach the dog to look left. One point to note about this cue is that it is important that you decide beforehand whether it is your left or your dog's left that is being cued. It is easier if you cue *"Left"* for the dog's left as it can be more confusing for us if we are behind the dog, cue *"Left"* and the dog looks right because when we taught the behaviour the dog was facing us and looking to our left.

1. With the dog sitting in front, lure the dog to look to it's left (your right). Click for any left movement, regardless of how small. Even the dog's eyes moving to the left can be clicked. Repeat a couple of times.

2. Wait for the dog to offer the behaviour even if only slightly. Click and reward.

3. Once the dog is offering the consistent behaviour, add the cue "Head Left" or "Left" depending where else you may want to use the Left cue.

HEAD RIGHT

In exactly the same way as for Look Left, teach the dog to look right. Remember to make it the dog's right, not yours so as not to make teaching confusing at a later date.

Sometimes when teaching the dog to look right or left we find that the dog turns its head but not its eyes - the eyes are still trying to face forwards looking at you. The dogs seem to be more dexterous to one way rather than both, so the behaviour looking to one way will be stronger than the other.

BODY MOVEMENTS

Many of the books in the Clicker Trainers Series by Kay Laurence (*from Learning About Dogs*) include recipes for getting the dog to move particular ways or specific body parts.

RECIPE 16

LAY ON SIDE WHEN CUED

For a dog, lying down on its side puts it in a very vulnerable position, however it also means that the dog is content and confident. For grooming this position is very calming (for both dog and groomer) and great for just about everything you need to do with the dog: blow-drying, brushing, combing, de-matting, clipping the nails, ear cleaning, the list goes on. The dog remains relatively still and will often even snooze while it is being groomed.

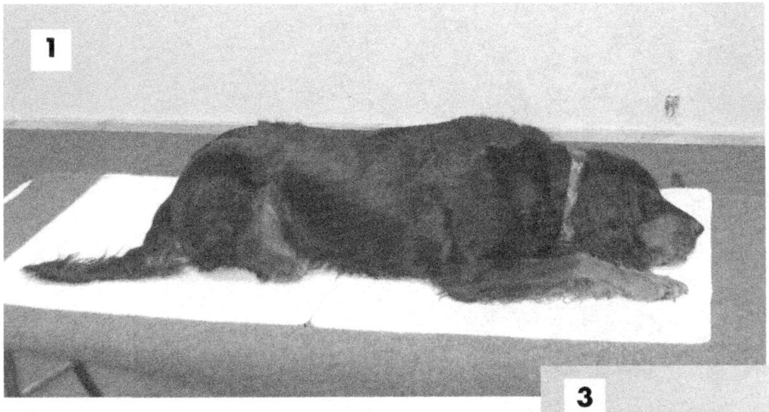

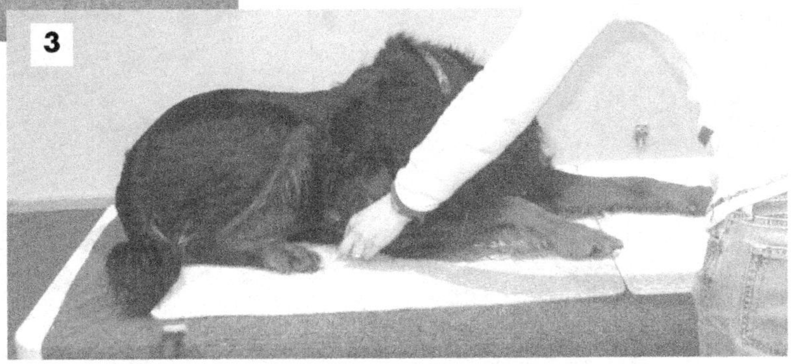

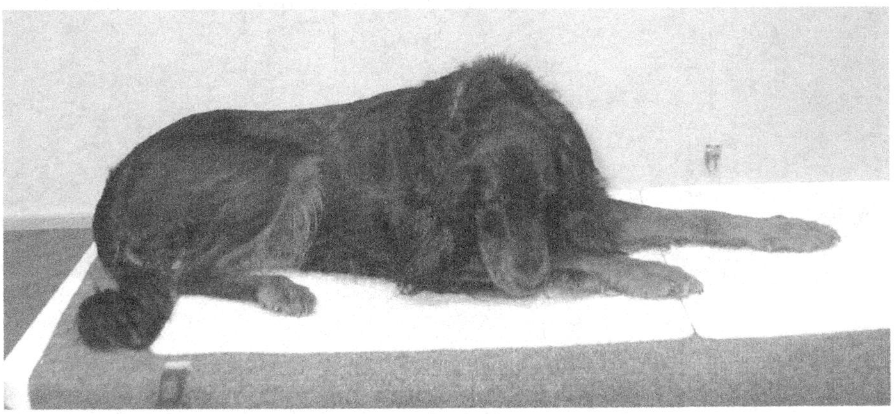

"settle"

1. Teach the dog to lay down, by either luring or by gradually clicking and rewarding the dog for lowering their head. The cue for this would be *"down"*

2. Once the dog is comfortable laying on the floor, continue to maintain this position by rewarding in position.

3. Teach the dog to settle their hips to one side by taking the treat to a point on the floor just behind their elbow. This forces the dog's spine to gently bend and the hips will roll to one side. The cue for this would be *"settle"*.

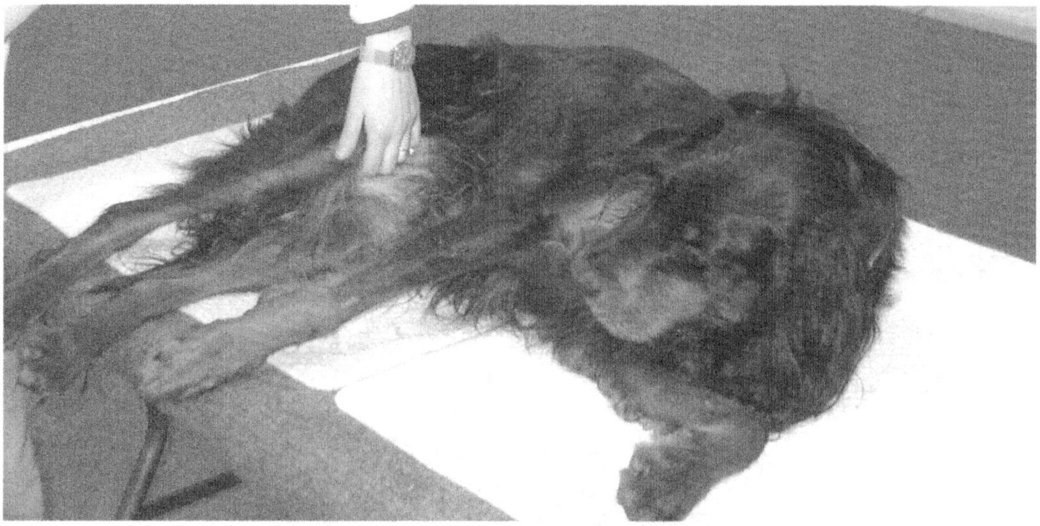

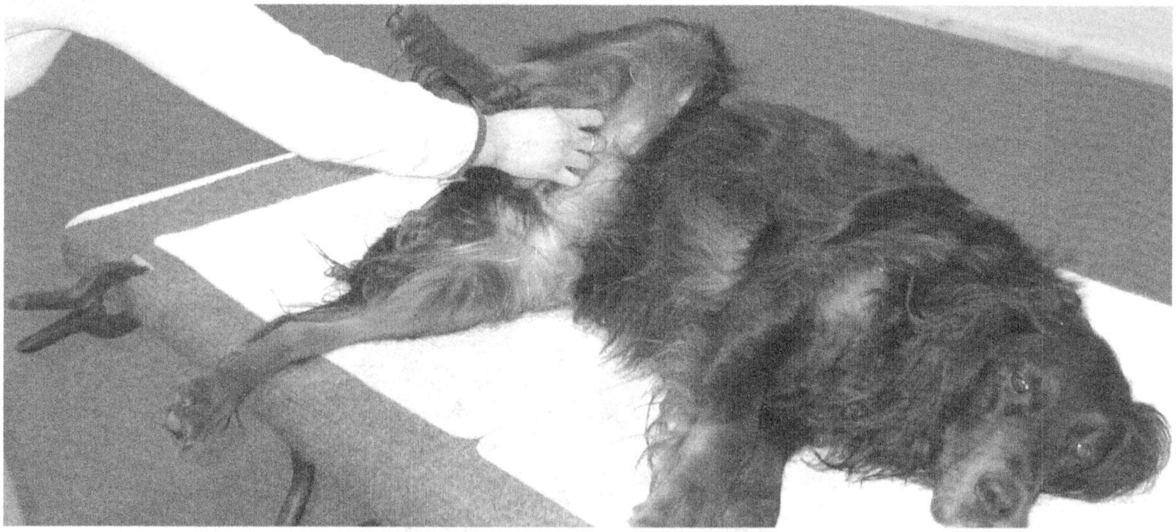

4. Continue taking the treat slightly further back and under the dog's chest to encourage them to roll onto one shoulder. Repeat the action of rolling onto one shoulder several times to gain confidence. If you want to repeat a movement, click and feed in the initial position and let the dog show you what movement they have learned. The cue for this would be *"roll"*

5 Once the dog is relaxed on their side, click and deliver the treats to the dog in this position.

6. To encourage the dog to lift their back leg, stroke gently just inside the up most leg, and they usually lift the leg. The cue for this would be *"show me"*

LAY ON BACK WHEN CUED

You could continue on with teaching the full rollover as outlined above, where the dog holds still while lying on its back - this is especially helpful for grooming the belly and groin area. Teach each position with separate cues so that the dog understands which position is required. The cue for this would be *"over"*

RECIPE 17

HOLD STILL

Essentially you are clicking the dog for standing still, or for no movement in the stand position. Using a nose to a target on a wall can be an effective way of giving the dog some action to start with and then maintaining that position once cued for varying lengths of time.

Begin this exercise with puppies during their daily grooming sessions. Firstly I teach them to stand squarely, with a leg at each corner, and groom with my hands. Plenty of stroking all around the body. You can use the click to mark the lack of movement and the stroke as the reward. Begin to build up the level of endurance through gradual tests of resistability to movement:

1. Lift one leg and click for balance maintained on three.
2. Gently stretch the tail and feel when the muscles resist, click for that resistance.
3. Put slight pressure along the spine, as soon as you feel the muscle push back, click and stroke.
4. Push gently on the flanks and shoulders and click for resisting a side step.

Build up the intrusive nature of the examination, check teeth, ears, under the tail. If your dog is particularly shy, teach them to seek contact, by shaping them to move their head into the palm of the approaching hand without leaving the position.

Be aware of the length of time the dog stays standing for, especially for older dogs - their bodies may not be physically capable of maintaining this behaviour for too long.

To be able to groom the back end of the dog, use a target to keep the dog facing away from you, and let the dog become familiar and confident with lots of handling from your hands initially, before you begin with equipment.

above: nose target to teach the dog to stand still

right: standing still for the automatic treat feeder.

RECIPE 18

LIFT FRONT PAWS OR LEGS

Many dogs will use their front legs in the same way we use our arms, to reach out and touch something. Using this behaviour and sustaining it gives us the ability to groom the front legs, trim nails and check feet without having to bend over the dog and with the dog offering its body part willingly.

- Sit on the floor with the dog, pot of food handy and clicker ready to go.
- With your free hand place a smelly piece in the centre of your palm and lightly close your fingers. Waft the hand via the dog's nose and place the back of your hand to the floor.
- Loosen the fingers so that the tongue can wiggle through and get a hint of the food.
- Dogs will usually use their mouth to try to get the food out, but with the frustration from lack of success they will try with their paw.
- The MINUTE the paw touches your hand, click, and spring the hand open for dog to collect the food. Do this three times.
- Go through the same sequence again but without food in the hand. Place the back of your hand to the floor and wait for the paw tap, click and with the signal hand collect and deliver a piece of food.
- Over the next few sessions when you give the signal, begin to open your fingers out so that the dog smacks the palm of your hand.

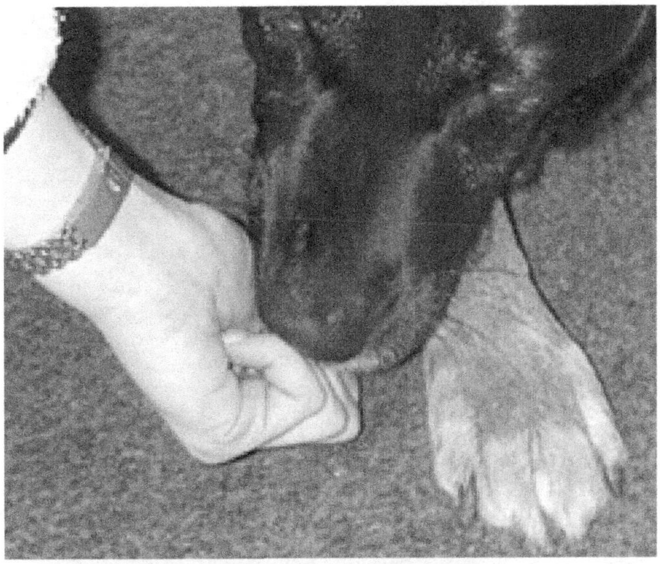

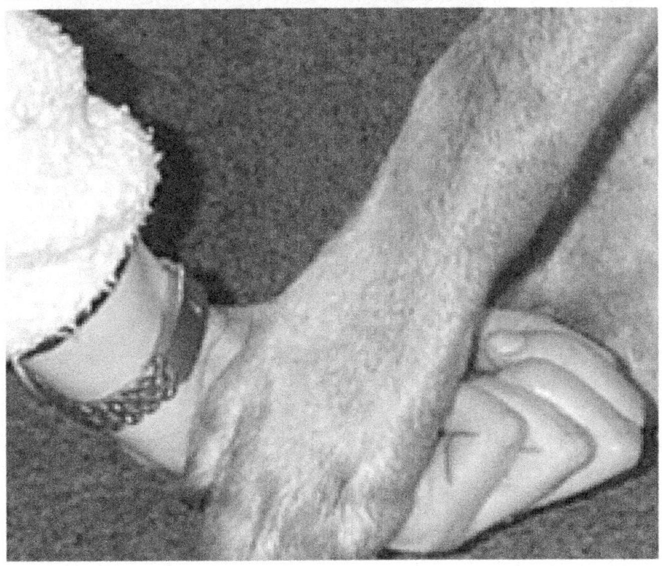

5 Clip, Brush and Trim

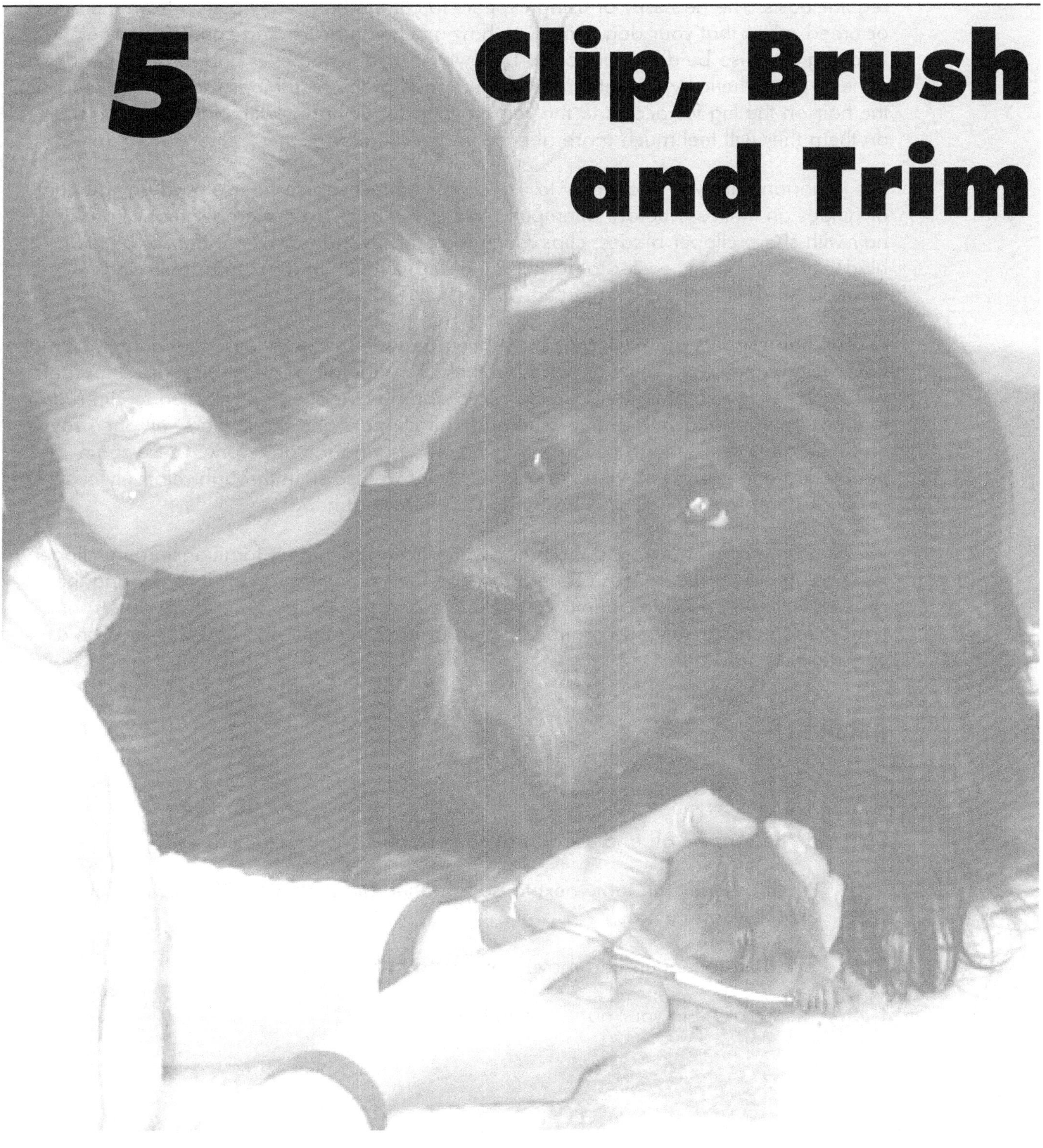

CLIPPING

Some dogs will never see or hear hair clippers, while others have to be clipped on a regular basis. The necessity of using clippers to cut the hair really comes from the breed or breed-mixes that your dog is or even how much you brush and comb your dog. Clipping can also be done for comfort. However if your dog ever had to be put under general anaesthetic by the veterinary surgeon one of the first things that is done is to clip the hair on the leg for access to the vein. If your dog is happy with clippers being used on them they will feel much more at ease in any situation.

It is important that you know how to use clippers effectively so please read any manual or guides on their use before attempting to clip the dog. Do remember that clean, dry hair with sharp clipper blades, clips much more easily than dirty, wet hair or blunt blades. If a process is easier to do, then the dog is much more comfortable and therefore less likely to be intimidated.

Animal hair clippers are best; they have been designed to work with animal hair. Human hair clippers may work once or twice but they are generally not fast or sharp enough to withstand the length of time it takes to clip a dog. I have often been called to clip a dog that has been started with ordinary human hair clippers and the owners will often say that the hair is really tough because they have tried and it didn't work. These same people are often surprised when the clippers that we use slide through relatively easy; but we are using professional tools designed for the task at hand.

We can use a similar recipe to the hair dryer introduction when familiarising the clippers, however the slight differences are that the dog feels the vibration on its body and the clippers will often need to go into very intimate areas of the dog, i.e. under the front legs, the tail and around the groin. Clipping around the face and ears can also be a very delicate procedure.

RECIPE 19

CLIPPERS

Start with the clippers off and clicking at each stage to reinforce them as a positive:

1. Put the clippers on table next to dog and let dog look at, sniff or investigate it. It's ok if the dog ignores it.

2. Pick the clippers up and move from hand to hand.

3. Then move it in your hand around the dog.

4. Turn the clipper on without a blade in it (if you are using a clipper that has detachable blades) and move around the dog in the same manner as before but without touching the dog.

5. Attach any blades or clipping combs to the clipper as required - all dependent on which brand of clipper that is being used.

6. Ask the dog to stand and perhaps target something to keep the dog still.

Where possible I start clipping the dog on either the back or rump, furthest from the head and ears as possible. This enables the dog to get used to the feel of the clippers on its body before you have to delve into those sensitive areas.

7. Whenever you begin clipping in a new place of the dog click and treat so that the dog is constantly being reinforced.

8. Repeat this whenever you ask the dog to turn or change to a new position.

Once the dog is comfortable with the process you can begin to reduce the level of clicking. The sound of the clippers themselves will become a familiar and positive association.

BRUSHING

Suzy, a colleague of mine, once told me that they use two brushes to brush their Labrador named Bella, one to use as her chew toy while the other brush performs the grooming function.

Many dogs don't like being brushed because it is often started when the dog really needs it and because they need it we tend to rush and force. This ends up either scaring the dog or making it believe that the brush is an evil owner-agitator. Other times we have made a game of brushing the dog so much that just like my colleague the dog just thinks the whole process is something to play with, and just won't stand or sit still during grooming. Sometimes we may feel guilty for letting our dog's coats get into disarray, and this guilt is transferred down the brush so that the dog feels that the whole process is best avoided.

Just like us, dogs have nerve endings in their skin and they will feel the pressure of a hard brush and the pull of a tangle. Some dogs seem to be sensitive to the lightest touch while others have a higher tolerance to any hair pulling that may occur. Whichever type of tolerance your dog has it is important to understand the thinking process that they may typically go through.

Like bathing the brushing sequence can often follow this procedure:

- × Get brush from cupboard or bench.
- × Call dog to us.
- × Go find dog.
- × Drag dog out from under the dining room table.
- × Take dog by collar to where you will brush it.
- × Physically lift or push dog into easiest grooming position, usually this is with both the dog and ourselves on the floor.
- × Brush dog - while also trying to hold dog in place.
- × Dog struggles and yelps and/or growls.
- × Other family member is yelled at to hold the dog in place while we vigorously brush the dog - for some reason we think that the harder we brush the quicker it gets done!
- × Dog is physically manhandled into another position in order to get to all body parts.
- × Dog still struggling, yelping and/or growling.
- × Owners relax hold on dog and dog escapes into the nether regions of the house.
- × Owner gives up and vows that once they finally get to brush the dog that they will do so more often!

So let's imagine another possible scenario:

- ✓ Get brush from cupboard or bench.
- ✓ No need to call dog to us dog heard us getting the brush and has come running.
- ✓ Brush dog asking the dog to turn, lift or wait as required in order to groom all over.
- ✓ Owner stops brushing dog after realising that they've both enjoyed it so much that they've continued the grooming session even though the dogs coat is beautiful again!

I have seen many a dog with beautiful gleaming upper coats that are tangle free, but delving underneath the top coat can often be quite a surprise to the owner as a second coat can be matted to the point where the dog's skin is probably not breathing very well, which can lead to health problems. This is one of the reasons why it is so important to not only make sure you brush under the top coat but using a comb that reaches to the skin can be just as important.

Many owners think that the matted hair is actually part of the dog's anatomy and don't realise what has happened to the undercoat. Even dogs without a full undercoat can get matted hair and knots, usually these are found in areas of the dog that are rubbed frequently - behind the ears, under the front legs, on the body where movement causes the leg to touch the body.

The simple act of rubbing your dog with a towel causes the hair to move which can cause matting, especially so if after being wet the dog then curls up to get warm.

I have assumed that your dog understands the basics such as sit, down, stand, wait and/or stay - if not then I suggest you teach these basics first so that they can be used during your grooming sessions. *(These Recipes can be found in the Clicker Trainers Series Foundation and Novice books from Learning About Dogs).* Even though the belief maybe that teaching your dog to stay is enough of a cue to enable grooming easily, the difference between staying willingly and staying because of dire consequence should be enough to give reason to teaching other cued behaviours.

To help your dog learn that being brushed can be a pleasant experience use the following recipes for the different behaviours.

So how do we get to the dog enjoying brushing? We need to start associating the brush and the feel of it as good. However, if your dog is badly matted with a coat in dire need of attention and is the type of dog that you can't get near with a brush then I would suggest that rather than working up to the perfect grooming pose that you take the dog to a professional who can work their magic on the dog. It may mean that the coat needs cutting back but whatever the case they will be able to give you a dog with a coat that you can start the positive grooming process with.

RECIPE 20

THE BRUSH

Using the tool association process will help a brush-fearing dog overcome the fear of the implement. When starting to use the brush I will generally follow similar guidelines as we used for introducing the hair dryer or clippers. However I believe it is more important that the dog knows what you are doing with the brush since it will need to be brushed from head to foot. I will often start with the dog sitting in front of me and use the brush lightly on the chest so the dog can watch me and I can watch the dog's reactions more easily.

1. With the dog sitting in front of you, hold the brush, click and treat.
2. Move the brush once downwards in front of the chest without actually touching the dog, click and treat.
3. Move the brush once downwards gliding over the chest slightly with the brush, click and treat.
4. Repeat 3-4 times.
5. Gradually increase the pressure of the brush on the dog's hair until you gently feel the dog's body, clicking and treating each time.

Remember to be mindful of the pressure that you are using, keep it gentle and glide over the dog's coat, the brush should not be forced into the hair or onto the body. Too often the brush is used too forcefully on the dog instead of being allowed to work on the hair as designed.

6. Add the cue "Brush" as you are brushing the dog. Click and treat every time the dog sits still while the brush touches him.
7. Gradually add more brush strokes between clicks.

Be careful of what you are clicking in that the behaviour is the dog being still and being brushed, and that other little behaviours aren't coming into play, like weight shifting and leg lifts.

8. After the dog is comfortable with you grooming the chest move the brush from the chest and over the shoulders. Click and treat.
9. Then from the chest, go over the shoulders and down the side of the dog. Click and treat.

Each time you move the brush to a new place on the dog, do so by going from a place the dog is happy with being brushed. The dog is able to feel the progress of the brush and will be much more comfortable.

10. The next step is to be able to perform the same with the dog standing and lying down. Introducing the turn cue during brushing will help you reach other parts of the dog without having to reach over it.

The process of brushing the whole dog's body can be achieved in either one session or over many sessions. Keep the process quick and simple and try to stop on success, this is equally important with a dog that has learned to hate being brushed as well as one that continually plays with the brush.

I have found that the optimum time for brushing the dog is in the evening after dinner, when the family has quietened down and relaxed. It is not advisable to teach the dog to enjoy being brushed when you are rushing to do something else or be in different places.

RECIPE 21

THE COMB

Once the brush has been successfully introduced, the comb can be used. Combs are essential in that they easily get to the skin level while parting the hair. However a comb will catch tangles and knots (depending on how wide the comb's teeth are set) so have more potential to pull skin. It is important that you keep the dog's skin taut and possibly even hold the hair between the knot and the skin so that the dog does not feel the isolated pressure point on its body.

Since the comb does generally touch the skin be careful to keep the pressure limited and not drag the comb too deeply over the skin, as this will be painful to the dog.

OTHER CUTE CUES

If you've taught your dog to fetch, name each of the grooming tools and cue your dog to fetch each one by name:

Fetch Brush

Fetch Comb

Fetch Towel

Fetch Clippers (nail clippers)

Fetch the Shampoo

Fetch Toothbrush - with this one I'd make sure only to name the dog's toothbrush and to keep it in a place away from the rest of the households'.

I wouldn't necessarily teach the dog to fetch electrical equipment, as your estimation of the cost of them is much higher than the dog's opinion of the same tools.

RECIPE 22

THE HAND-STRIPPER

The hand-stripping tool removes the dead hair from the coat that does not come out with brushing or combing and does so without actually cutting the hair. The same can be achieved but using a plucking type action with your fingers and thumb but takes a lot longer than using the correct tool.

1. When you first introduce the dog to hand stripping ensure that you start off with light almost non-existent pulling but click and treat every time the dog relaxes when you pull.

2. Gradually increase the intensity so that the dog gets familiar with the feel of the hair being tugged. Be careful to click for the standing still and relaxing, not for pulling away from what is being done.

Correct stripping should not cause the dog any pain.

TRIMMING

If your dog is longhaired, likes being groomed and is groomed regularly, then trimming is usually a fairly easy task. Just ask the dog to lift a paw to trim those excess hairs between the toes, separate the toes and carefully trim - ideally the dog stays very still and doesn't mind how long you take to trim and can handle a bit of poking and prodding by you in locating where the hair ends and the skin begins. Or even just ask them to stand still so that a neat finishing effect of their under belly hair (skirt) or the hair at the end of their ears and tail are trimmed neatly.

We're also breeding more dogs now that have hair that doesn't fall out, but if it doesn't fall out then it will need trimming or clipping. And some breeds grow lots of facial hair that ends up impeding their eyesight and can become an irritant because of this.

Many dogs do not sit still when they are being groomed and this is especially dangerous (for both human and canine alike) when we have a pair of scissors in our hand. I know many an owner who has confessed to accidentally cutting their dog when trying to remove knots or burrs from their dog's coat. Ask any vet to tell you how many times they stitch up wounds from owners trying to trim the hair on their dog. So the importance of trimming and using scissors is not to be taken lightly.

Dogs being the body language creatures that they are can easily tell when a scissor-operator is not adapt at using the implement or if that person is nervous or frustrated about getting the knots out of the dog's coat. And the dog reacts accordingly! I know I certainly wouldn't sit still if a scissor-wielding hairdresser was shaking or acting apprehensive before cutting my hair!

Important points:

- Make sure the dog is happy with the implement that you are going to use, especially around the face.
- If you have a fidgety dog it is important that you are dexterous enough to move with the dog and able to stop yourself cutting in mid-stroke.
- Familiarise yourself with the safest method of using the scissors so as to prevent a cut occurring should the dog move suddenly.

USING SCISSORS

Whatever part of the coat that needs trimming, ensure you have a good solid behaviour from the dog that will ensure it remains still. This may mean that you need to use your imagination and get the dog to try a few different positions for optimum accessibility and use. Rather than being frustrated, think of it as a challenge and have some fun luring or shaping the dog into different positions. Sometimes a hand on another part of the body will help keep the dog still, but be sure to only place your hand rather than grabbing and holding, I try to use my hand more as a guide than a grabbing instrument.

Using a nose touch to a target or asking the dog to perform the **HEAD ON** *(Recipe 14 Page 48)* behaviour can help keep a dog's head still while you trim around the mouth, nose, ears or eyes.

When using scissors ensure you know exactly what you are cutting, many dogs end up with matted hair in very hard reaching places i.e. at the top inside part of the front legs and around the pelvic area to name a couple. But even if the area is not hard to reach, where the hair starts and the skin ends can be difficult to determine. I have seen a number of dogs with cuts around their ears because the owner tried to remove matted hair behind the ear.

Some dogs can become what seems phobic when the scissors come out, especially if they are moved near the eyes, as mentioned before, try relaxing before attempting any scissoring on your dog, and introduce them in the same way you would for any other unknown tool so that the dog is allowed to become confident around them. I know I wouldn't be confident if the hairdresser had a shaky hand with something foreign in it when approaching me, especially to cut my hair!

6 Regular care and treatment

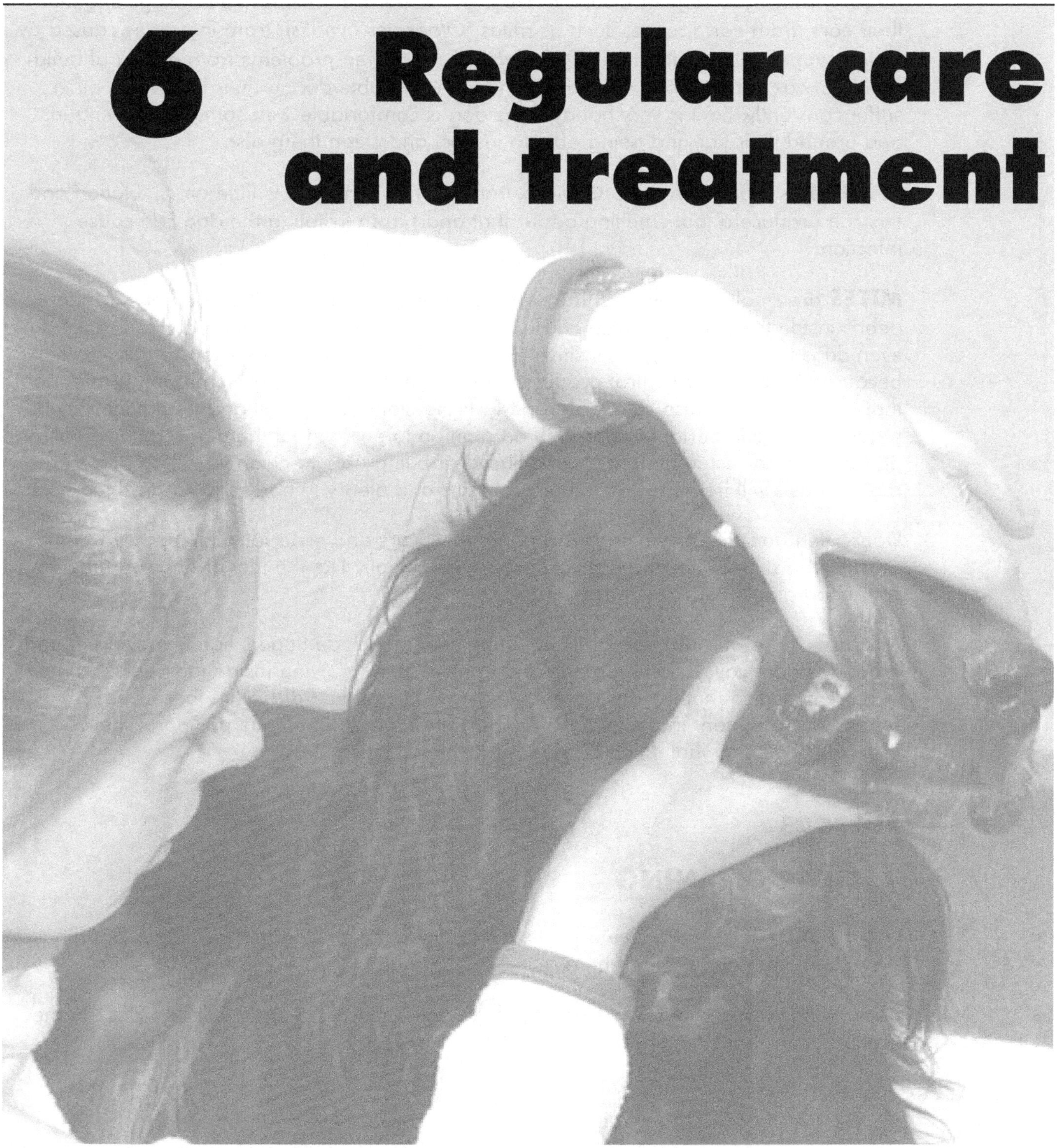

CLEANING EARS

All dogs need their ears checked regularly and depending on the type of ears your dog has they may need regular cleaning. Dogs can suffer from items like seeds getting into their ears, from ear diseases such as mites (*Otodectes cynotis)*, from infections caused by water trapped in the ear canal (*Otitis Externa)*, and even problems from a natural build-up of earwax . Some dogs can have minimal ear trouble during their lives while others suffer constantly. So it is very handy if the dog is comfortable with someone playing in and around their ear and being able to inspect and clean them also.

CANKER is a build-up of natural wax that occurs when there is little air circulation and this can produce a foul-smelling odour that apart from irritating the dog can cause infection.

MITES are small white insects that cause a dark brown to black build up of wax-like debris inside the ear. They often cause the dog to shake its head and ears constantly but even dogs that are not hypersensitive to the itching can end up with severe ear infections because of them. Flea control products can help eliminate the problem but it is important that the dog's ear is also cleaned properly. Professional diagnosis and treatment may be required and is important to get such an opinion to ensure that the dog remains healthy and that the correct treatment occurs. However being able to clean your dog's ears on a regular basis will help prevent future problems and alert you early should anything occur.

Dogs often don't like anything being put in their ears and especially liquid, they will move away at the slightest touch. And yet some dogs actually like the feel of fingers in the ears or a good gentle ear rub on the outside.

As a dog is growing up, part of its handling should include fingers lightly moving in and around the ear cavity. Some breeds of dog have hairs growing inside their ears that need to be removed so that the ear doesn't clog up with wax and dirt. With these types of breeds it is important that they become fairly immune to the gentle pulling of their internal ear hair so that it can be removed without stress.

RECIPE 23

EAR CLEANING

Use the **TOUCH ME** (*Recipe 3 page 20)* to first get your dog used to hands and fingers manipulating in and around the ear.

Be careful that you click away from the dog's ear - the sound of the click so close to the eardrum can cause damage.

With my own Gordon Setters that need regular ear care, Vienna prefers to lie on a target mat on the floor, whilst Connor prefers to stand and rest his chin on a soft toy as a target.

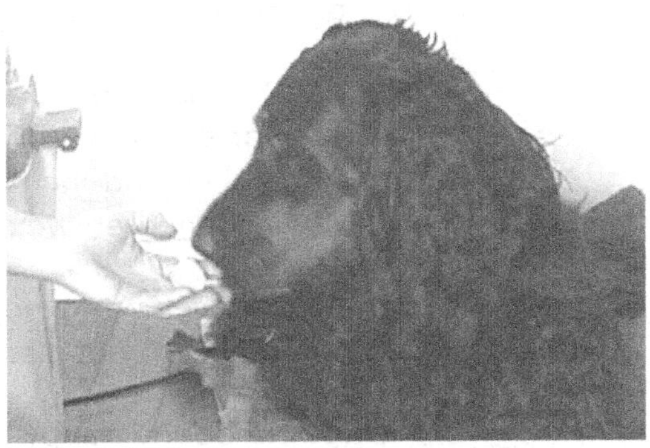

Before using clicker training to teach the dog about happy ear cleaning I would usually have the dog sitting between my legs while I leaned over the top of them to hold their head and body still and to try and manipulate the cotton wool, the cleaner and their ear at the same time.

The method I found the easiest for both myself and the dog was that of Connor's and using the **HEAD ON** (*Recipe 14 page 48)* . Vienna's method was to use the clicker as a confidence-enforcer of accepting the touch and cleaning rather than that of a separate action, so the method below starts with acceptance and then goes into the co-operation of working together to get the end result.

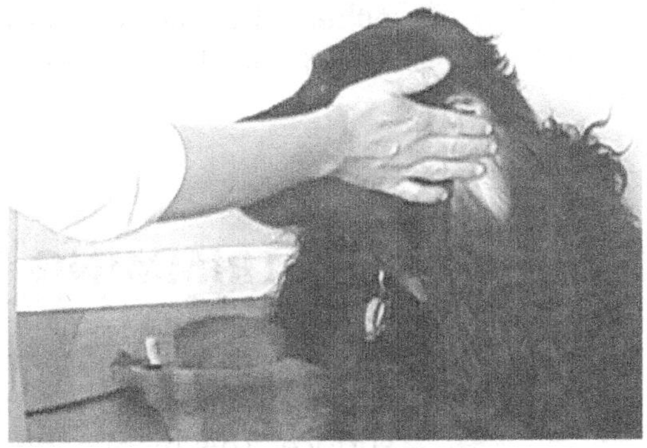

1. With the dog in a comfortable position in front of you, gently touch the inside of its ear, click and treat.

2. Take a small piece of cotton wool or similar material, and gently touch the inside of the ear with it, click and treat. Repeat a few times.

3. Let the dog sniff the bottle of ear cleaner and touch the bottle to the ear, click and treat.

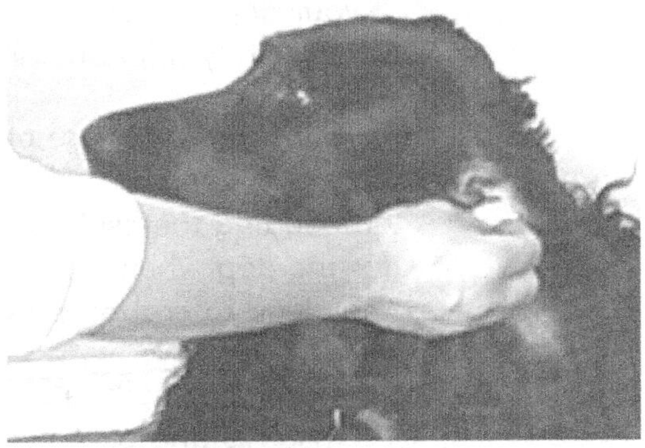

4. Put a tiny bit of ear cleaning lotion onto a ball of cotton wool and gently wipe the inside of the ear, starting with the ear-flap and moving down to just inside the ear. Click and treat.

   Do not soak the cotton wool, just enough for the dog to feel the temperature change.

5. Put more lotion on the ball of cotton wool so that a tiny bit of excess liquid may run into the ear. Continue to gently wipe the ear at the same time so that not too much goes too far into the canal.

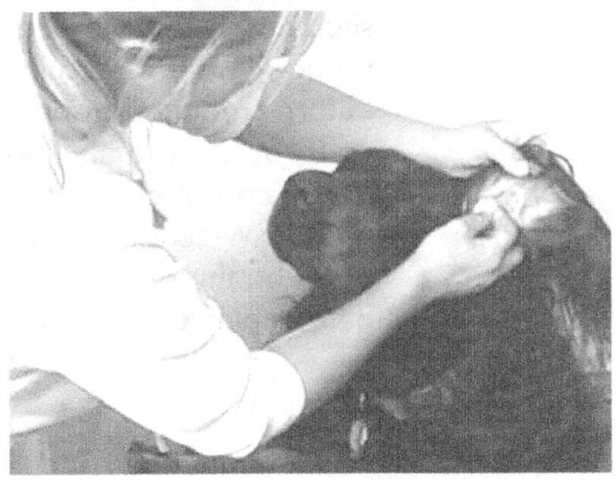

You should be clicking and treating throughout the different steps of the process so that the dog associates the ear interference in a positive manner.

6. Put a few drops of the ear cleaner into the ear canal, ensure you click and treat.
7. With the cleaner inside the ear you need to gently massage the base of the dog's ear so that you hear a type of squishy sound, allow the dog to shake its head if it wishes and then use the cotton wool to gently wipe out the excess liquid and loosened earwax.

The above steps may need to be done over a period of time because it is important not to put too much ear cleaning fluid into the dog's ear canal in any one session.

Once the dog is happy accepting you touching the ear, inside and out, and of the ear being cleaned then continue on to teach the "Head On" action and use this behaviour either on an item that both you and the dog can reach easily or even ask the dog to target your lap or something on your lap.

TRIMMING NAILS

Many dogs will wear their nails down naturally on hard surfaces but if your dog is like mine, they spend more time running around on a soft park rather than on a hard surface. This means that they will need their nails trimmed on a more regular basis.

If your dog has dew claws these may only touch the ground when the dog is at a full run which rarely happens on the hard surfaces so they may need more regular attention.

If your dog's nails are allowed to continue growing and they are not being worn down naturally, eventually they may split, tear off or even grow too long and curl around, embedding themselves into the dog's foot pad. Apart from causing general discomfort for the dog when walking or running this could lead to infection and pain, which in turn may lead to crabbiness or worse.

Trimming the nails is probably the one area that many owners are not confident in doing themselves and as a consequence, the dog learns that something is not right about the situation so learn to fear the event. On top of this the nail clippers or grinders can often be noisy when operating and this noise is associated with pressure on the nail; which can in turn create an apprehensive connection for the dog. There are a few ways to trim nails, by using nail clippers that cut the nail, by using a nail file and filing the nail down or this can also be done with an electric file specifically built to sand the nails down quickly. Whichever tool you use be sure to understand how it works before attempting to use it on the dog. It is also important to know the parts of the nail so that this task can be completed with minimal fuss.

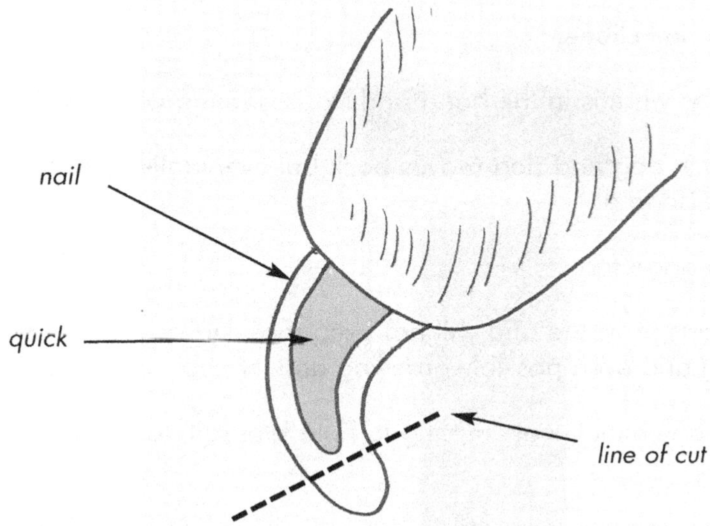

The quick is the name for the blood vessel that runs down part of each nail, if when trimming the dog's nail the quick is cut, it will bleed. If cut too often the dog will associate the act of nail trimming as a painful event which understandably can cause the dog to fear nail trimming. Just like the human nail, the end of the outer shell has no nerves so as long as it is only the end of the nail that is trimmed, the act of cutting the nail will not be felt, which is again just like for human nails.

Ideally the dog would offer its foot and spread its toes so that each toenail can be checked and administered as necessary - all this while either staying still, not reacting to the sound of the clippers and also repositioning itself on cue in order to make the job easier for you to do.

However many dogs may flinch or pull away when we pick up their foot and some may even yelp in surprise, and we can end up struggling with the dog in order to complete the task. Eventually we give up as the struggle either stresses us, the dog or both. Because dogs learn very quickly if something they do stops an anticipated course of action from continuing, they then learn that yelping, whining or struggling will cause us to stop trying to trim their nails. It may be that the dog has never really had anything happen to it during nail clipping, only that the dog has learnt that for some reason this is an action that isn't right as everyone in the family gets upset during this event.

Scenarios that I have seen happen may follow this procedure:

1. Having learnt from previous grooming attempts we locate the dog first and bring it into a room first.
2. Pick up nail clippers.
3. Dog sees what is in the hand and starts panting while pacing around the room.
4. Approach dog and dog moves back but eventually stops (by a wall as there is no where else to go).
5. Pick up dog's foot.
6. Dog starts to writhe and will not keep foot, leg or even body still, still whining and panting and even possibly growling and/or showing teeth.
7. After many minutes attempting to hold foot still, lay dog in the down position on side.
8. Physically lay human body on top of dog to hold it in position and get someone else to clip the nails - during this time dog is still writhing and is probably whining, panting hard and trembling.
9. Remove body from on top of dog and dog runs away, owner ends up stressed or upset.

Most scenarios often end at point 6 but some will often end at either point 3 or 4. No one likes to see his or her dog stressed and this situation could easily lead to a more dangerous level because we force our course of action on the dog, in a highly stressful and vulnerable situation.

We took the same dog that gave us the above scenario and changed it into the following:

1. Pick up nail trimmers and call dog to us.
2. Dog comes, sits quietly in front of us and offers each paw in turn while nails are trimmed.
3. Dog gets reward at end.

The following recipe shows how we turn a once fearful dog into one that actually enjoys having nails trimmed.

RECIPE 24

NAILS

I would normally teach this with the dog in the sit position, but doing it from the stand and down positions can be just as effective. Ask for the paw taps with the front feet only - generally dogs are more nervous about what they see you doing so once they have mastered getting their front nails clipped they usually don't care about you doing the back feet.

1. Teach the dog to offer its paw to either you or a small target. You need to decide which before you start but you can transfer later on.

2. The dog needs to offer the paw and push onto the target so that the behaviour is solid. Click and reward for extra effort made in pushing and maintaining a hold with the paw.

You could get the dog to target a ball and hold its foot on it - this would have the effect of spreading the toes out naturally. Or alternatively if the dog is standing on a bench or table ask the dog to target the edge so that its toes are just hanging over the edge, this has the effect of spreading the toes out but the pressure is maintained naturally by the weight of the dog.

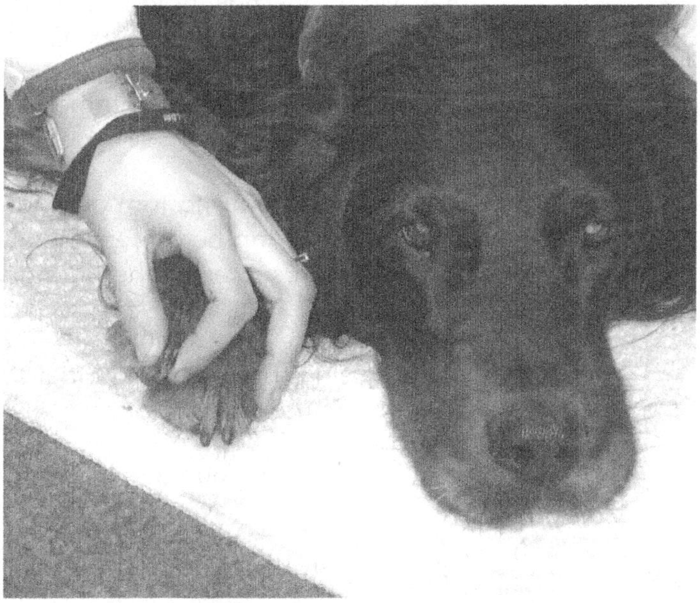

holding the nail in preparation for clipping, with the head target to the table

If I have a dog that hates having its feet touched asking them to give the paw allows them the liberty of making the decision, which grows confidence.

3. With the dog maintaining a paw hold, use the other hand to touch each toe and nail individually, click and reward for each touch.

4. Repeat for all toes and nails. When you move from one leg to another make sure you stroke the dog from one leg to the other so that it can feel where you are going.

> **Tip**
>
> If you accidentally cut the nail's quick, use soap to clog up the nail and apply pressure to the wound to stop the bleeding. It is probably equivalent to us getting a minor cut on our hand, hurts initially but with no major artery having been severed. If bleeding persists seek veterinary attention.

Some dogs freak out when touched suddenly, especially if they are not confident with foot touches.

5. Pick up the nail trimmers (clippers or sander type) with one hand and ask the dog for a paw hold to the other hand or target.
6. Raising the criteria is to ask the dog to target the trimmers, either while you are holding them or on top of the target mat.
7. While the dog is targeting the trimmers, repeat steps 3 & 4 above. Click and reward for the dog's foot remaining still.
8. Ask for the paw hold and touch each nail with the trimmers, in the off position for the sander type trimmers. Click and reward for stillness.
9. For those with noisy trimmers, repeat step 8 with them turned on - without using them.
10. The next step is to trim one nail at a time and click and reward for each one, ask for a paw tap before each nail is trimmed. It is best to trim a little bit at a time and gain success rather than try a complete nail clip and risk trimming the quick too.

If you are using a sander or grinder then ensure you do not press too hard or keep the sander on the nail for too long.

11. Now add in your cue of "Nails" so that the dog learns it is different from the paw tap. Raise the criteria to two nails, then a whole foot before clicking and rewarding.

When training the nail clipping behaviour it is best to take your time in going from one step to the next.

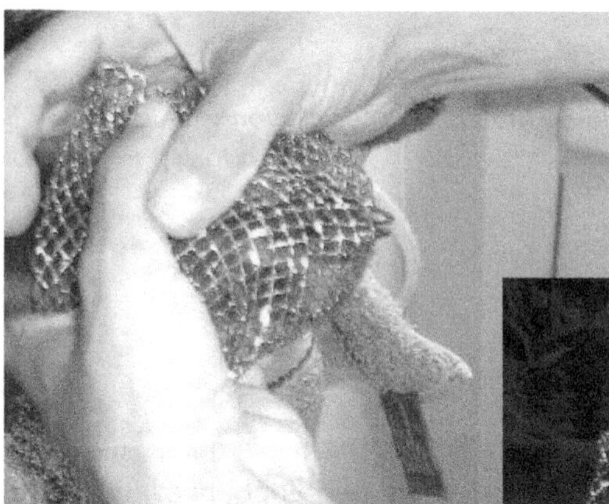

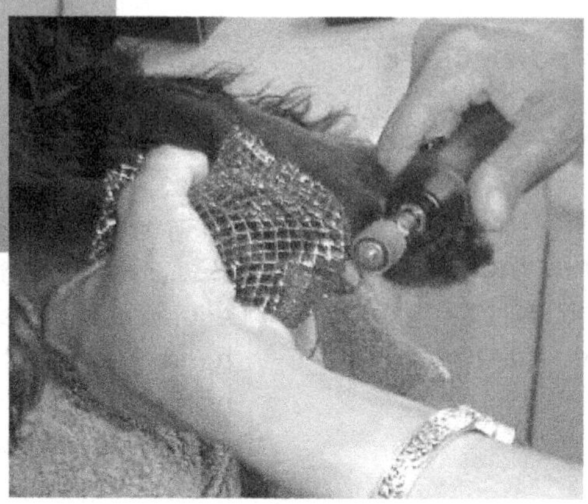

Tip

For a dog with lots of hair between their toes, try using a netting material (like an onion bag) and put around the foot so that only the nails show through the net, especially good for use with a sander/grinder that can catch excess hair in the spinning tool.

DENTAL CARE

There's a reason why the phrase "dog breath" has been used to describe an unpleasant odour emitting from someone's mouth! If the dog's teeth and gums are cared for the sweeter smelling their breath will be and the longer their teeth will last. I used to brush Guinness's teeth on a monthly basis and most of his teeth stayed strong and white right up until his passing at nearly 14 years of age. One of the reasons why dogs end up with foul smelling breath is the build up of tartar on their teeth and gums, if left to accumulate this tartar will eventually rot the dog's teeth and its the rotting smell that gives off the foul stench. Dog's also have a wonderful habit of panting when just at the right height so that you can make full use of this mouth odour!

Healthy teeth and gums also play an important part in the health and welfare of the dog, and there's no reason why your dog can't learn to have his or her teeth brushed and the mouth checked on a regular basis.

Nowadays it is possible to buy your dog a canine designed toothbrush and toothpaste from either your local veterinary clinic or pet supplies shop. The toothbrush has a longer handle so that you can reach the back of the longer muzzled dogs, and the toothpaste is flavoured for a more accepting taste to the dog. However using an old toothbrush of your own and water is better than not cleaning their teeth at all. Many dogs clean their teeth naturally by chewing on bones; biscuits and other similar products that are specifically designed to help ease the tartar build up on their teeth.

Teaching your dog to "smile" or lift its lips is one way of getting the dog to actively participate in brushing its teeth. But if your dog has long dewlaps then the act of lifting the side lips may not be as physically possible so it may be easier to teach your dog to hold its head still and be comfortable with you inserting hands, fingers and other items into its mouth. However teaching your dog to hold something in its mouth while being comfortable with you playing in its mouth is another way of ensuring your dog will be happy with you brushing its teeth.

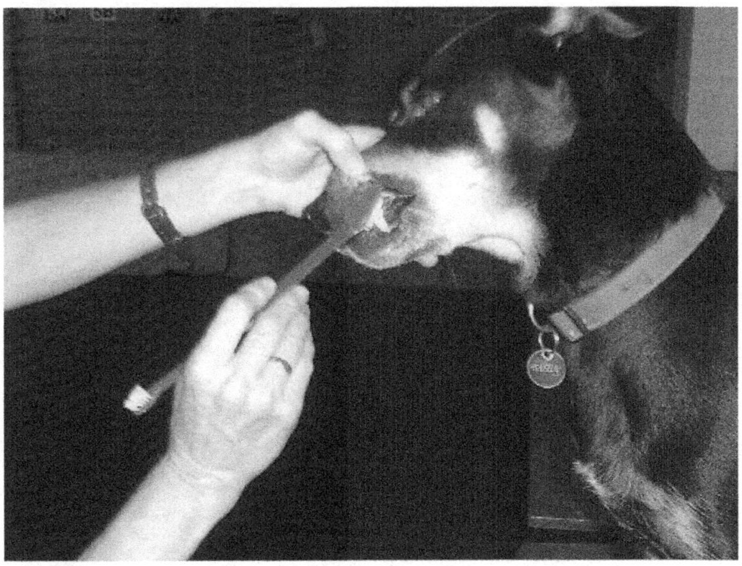

Using the food reward in clicker training already lets the dog become familiar in a highly positive way to hands being close to their mouth but often a dog will shy away from a hand getting any more familiar so the recipe below shows how to get your dog happy with you getting intimate with its mouth, and also with you using tools in its mouth.

This exercise can also help the owner overcome any fear of the dog and its mouth and teeth. It seems fairly common for humans to be scared of the dog's teeth and mouth and because of the power they have it is understandable. But dog's also have huge control over their body parts and if taught that there is nothing to fear in associating human hands with their mouth will have absolutely no reason to use their teeth threateningly. I liken it to humans having arms and hands, having the potential to use them in not such a nice manner to others but also having the instinct and/or training to know how to use hands in a friendlier manner. If you look at it another way, dogs known to each other can often lick at each other's mouths, take items such as toys from each other or even hold onto the same article with noses touching, and in all these instances the dog doesn't bite the other dog. In the same sense dogs will learn to accept human hands too.

RECIPE 25

MOUTH CHECK

1. If you have taught the dog to **HEAD ON** Recipe 14 page 48 using its mouth or muzzle, cue it to do this behaviour while holding your hand out just in front of you (the dogs needs to come very close if we are going to be successful in cleaning its teeth).

2. To ensure that the dog is a willing participant keep your hands a good distance apart and cue the dog to move its mouth towards one hand (the one that will touch the mouth and teeth) and hold the clicker and treats in the other hand.

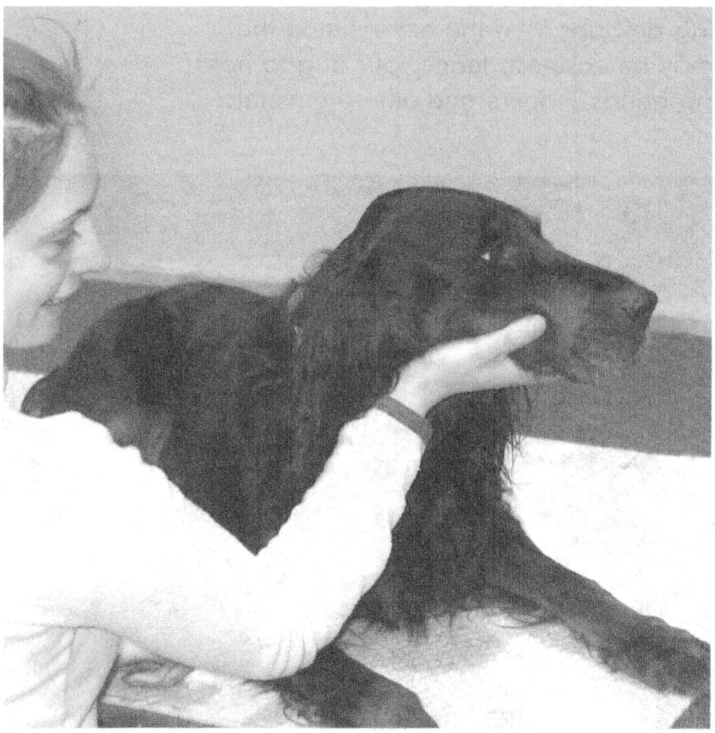

The dog is then repeating the action of moving its head from one hand to the other hand.

3. If you haven't taught the Touch behaviour initially click the dog for touching your hand. Quickly raise the criteria so that the dog keeps its head touching your hand for longer periods.

Just before you click use a release word so that the dog learns to wait until that release cue before moving its head away from your hand.

4. While the dog is holding its head against your hand gently extend your fingers and place them underneath the dogs dew flaps. Click, release and treat.

5. The next step is to wiggle your fingers against your dog's teeth, click, release and treat.

6. Repeat the above procedures but raise the criteria so that you go further around the outside of your dog's teeth, touching more teeth before you click and release.

7. Add the cue "*Teeth*" before you touch the teeth so that the dog can learn that this cue means you are about to touch the inside of its mouth. The dog may also move its teeth to touch your fingers, which is worth clicking.

Try to ensure the click happens for you touching, not for the dog moving away or even mouthing. Our requirement here is for the dog to be happy with us playing in the mouth, but for us to also be confident that the dog is not going to bite down.

8. Raising the criteria also includes extending the time period that you are playing or touching the teeth. Ensure that you separately train the time extension and the touching of more items inside the mouth.

4

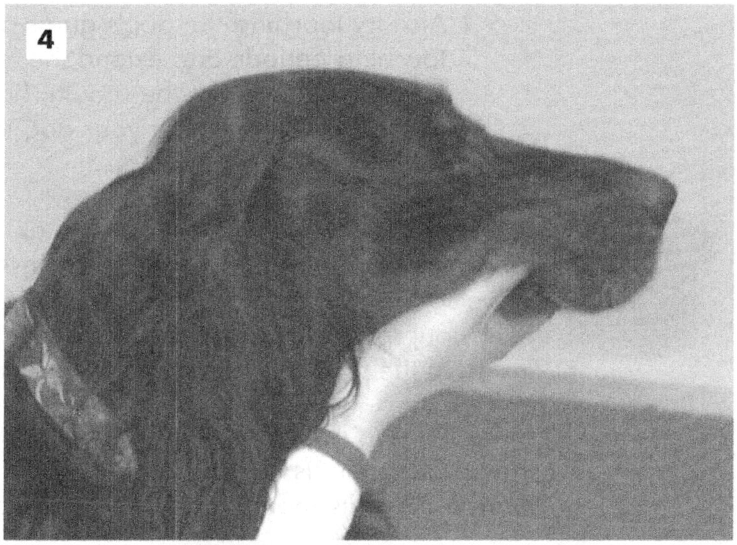

5

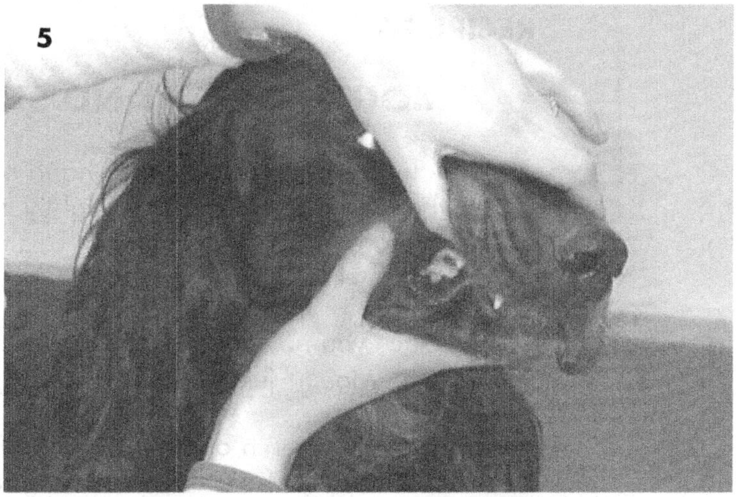

5

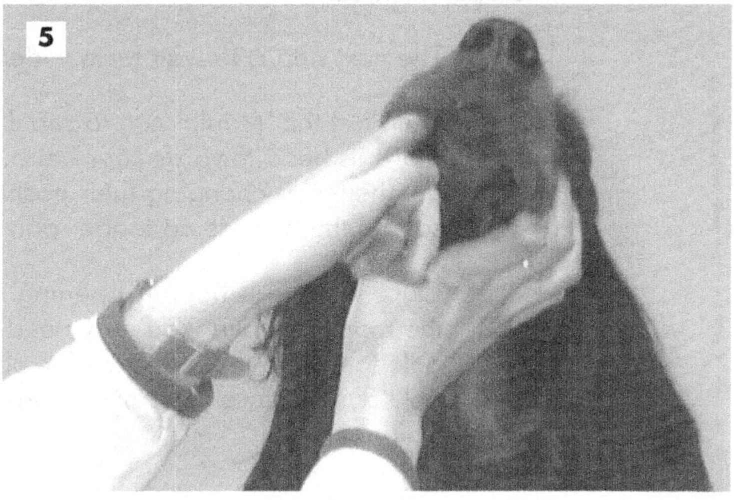

9. Also try touching the dog's gums and tongue, as with the teeth start with short touching periods and extend the length of time. The cue "Teeth" could be generic to all inside parts of the mouth, however this depends on how specific you would like to get with training your dog to understand its teeth from its tongue separately.

Remember to raise these criteria over as many sessions that the dog requires in order to be comfortable with you touching the inside of its mouth. Raise the criteria but do not move so fast that the dog gets worried about what you are doing. At this stage the behaviour to the dog becomes hold your mouth to the hand, and the touching of the inside of the mouth becomes a secondary action. The dog is waiting for a release signal.

Once the dog is comfortable with its mouth being touched inside then we want to teach the dog to open its mouth on cue without having to touch our hand to do so, and eventually to keep its mouth open until we release it.

RECIPE 26

MOUTH OPEN (AND SHUT)

1. After the dog touches your hand but before you begin to touch the teeth, click for the mouth opening, even slightly is great. The dog will generally anticipate what you are about to do and will begin to open its mouth, which gives us an opportunity to click.

2. Once you have got the dog opening its mouth consistently then begin to add the cue *"Mouth"* just before the dog opens its mouth. Remember to click and treat.

At this stage the mouth opening and the checking inside the mouth are two separate behaviours. Try to refrain from checking inside the mouth while you are teaching the dog to open its mouth.

3. The next step is to wait for a wider opening of the mouth before clicking.

4. Then test the "Mouth" cue to see if the dog will open its mouth without having to move its head towards your hand. Initially keep your hands in the same position but then start changing their position, usually by lowering them towards your side so that the hand is no longer part of the cue.

5. Once the dog is happily opening its mouth on cue, try adding a teeth touch while the mouth is open. You may need to go back to short touches initially but will be able to extend the number of teeth you touch and the time taken to do so reasonably quickly since you have already taught the dog to be comfortable with this action.

6. Another aspect to this is to cue the dog to close its mouth. Add a cue such as "Shut" just before the mouth action starts to close and click appropriately.

This could also be handy for keeping the dog quiet "Mouth"; "Shut" together!

The end test to know if the dog understands the cues, is whether the dog will open its mouth when you cue it, not close it until you ask, allow you to touch the teeth, gums and tongue while its mouth remains open and wait until you give the release cue before moving away.

We now want to start adding tools into our hands to use in our dog's mouth.

Ensure you let the dog familiarise itself with any utensils you intend to use, don't overdo it otherwise you may scare the dog with the "she's being weird about something again" behaviour. In the following instance I will introduce using a toothbrush, but the method applies to any other mouth utensil that needs to be used, such as a tartar scraper or even a pill popper or worming solution given in a syringe.

RECIPE 27

BRUSH TEETH

1. Hold the toothbrush in your hand without any part of it being extended. Cue the "Mouth" and "Teeth" behaviours, click and treat.

2. Then extend the toothbrush in your hand so that only a small part of it is showing. Cue "Mouth" and "Teeth", touch the toothbrush to the teeth, click and treat.

3. Keep repeating while extending the toothbrush in small increments. Be careful to make sure that the behaviour is of the toothbrush touching the teeth and gums and not for the dog mouthing it, nothing worse than trying to brush your dogs teeth while it is trying to eat the toothbrush.

4. In the same manner as for your hand in the dog's mouth, start moving the tooth-brush over the teeth before you click.

5. Keep raising the criteria so that the toothbrush is in the dog's mouth, and brushed across the teeth for longer periods before clicking.

6. The next step is to add a liquid onto the toothbrush and repeat the above steps.

I would start with water so that the taste difference is minimal and then introduce the toothpaste, first by letting the dog sniff and lick it before putting it on the toothbrush. It is possible to buy doggy toothpaste; it is usually flavoured so that the dog finds it reasonably appealing.

7. Once the dog is happily accepting its teeth being brushed I would introduce the cue "*Brush Teeth*"; this is effectively chaining the behaviours together and creating a new cue.

Keeping the cues for Mouth and Brush Teeth different will help the dog differentiate between you just opening their mouth and actually brushing their teeth.

ANAL GLANDS

Dogs have an anal (scent) gland or sac on each side of the anus. They allow the dog to mark territory when they defecate, but can sometimes empty when the dog is under pressure from fear. Some dogs however have a problem with their glands emptying naturally (impacted anal glands) so it is important that the glands are emptied manually.

If your dog is prone to blocked anal glands, speak with your veterinary staff and ask them to teach you how to empty them on a regular basis.

RECIPE 28

PILL POPPING

Giving a dog oral medication including worm tablets can sometimes be a painful experience for both owner and dog alike. When our dogs are young they require a mass cocktail of all sorts of medication, thankfully the veterinarian gets to administer most of the medicines via syringe but inevitably at some point in our dog's lives we will need to administer oral medication to them.

The first time you ever give your dog a pill it is important that they believe it is something yummy or never get to know that medication is being administered. When I was growing up we were taught that to give a dog a pill, you opened up their mouth and shoved the pill down their throat as quickly and as far as possible, then hold the mouth closed and keep a hand on the throat to make sure they swallowed - no wonder the dogs hated pill time!

A couple of ways to easily administer pills to your dog:

- Put the pill inside something yummy - a ball of cheese or mince. Give this to the dog as a treat, ask it to do something first and don't let your body language give away that you need the dog to swallow this. Dogs are smart - they know via your body language if something is not quite right!

- If you have a clicker savvy dog, then ask it to do some training, give treat, treat, treat, pill, treat, and treat! Generally the dog takes the pill and swallows before realising that it wasn't quite the treat it was used to.

- Offer the dog the pill outright - it may surprise you and just take and swallow - especially good for greedy canines!

By including this as part of your regular training sessions you can avoid ever having to jam pills down a dog's throat.

RECIPE 29

WEIGHT

Have you noticed that when you take your dog to the vet now that they insist the dog gets on the scales? Pretty good really as it means that you and your vet can keep an eye on your dog's weight and put the dog on a plan to adjust accordingly if necessary.

The local vet that I use has put the scale beneath the floor and covered it in exactly the same material as the rest of the floor - the dogs never even know they are being weighed - I however have to be careful where I stand!

Another vet that I work nearby has the scales on the floor but with an upright board on one side and on the end to make a corner - perhaps this is to ensure the dog doesn't walk off once on.

And yet another one has the scale on the floor beside a wall so that the dog just walks on and off at leisure.

Of the three types I actually think it's easier for the dog to have the scales showing but without any wall around it. Via clicker training the scales are more obvious to the dog and a clicker confident dog will investigate something like this quite readily. For the more nervous dog the scale in the floor is better as the dog doesn't realise why it's standing or sitting where it is - however trying to manipulate it to sit or stand in the right spot is sometimes tricky so using a target mat on the area is the easiest way to solve that problem.

Regardless of how the scales are shown take your clicker and treats to where the scale is and teach your dog to stand, sit or down in the right spot or on the right target. It is important that the dog also maintains the position for at least 30 seconds in order to get the correct reading.

A more common method is to use your own bathroom scales at home, with a small dog you can teach them to target and wait on the scales while you read them. With a bigger dog, you may need to hop on the scales yourself, read the measurement, then pick the

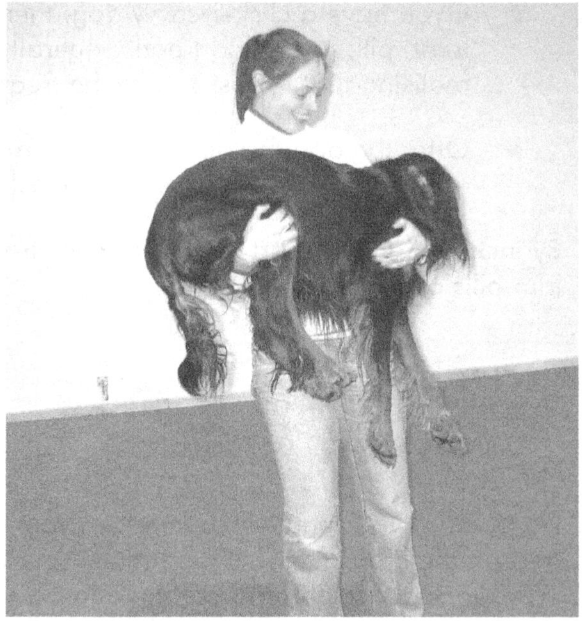

dog up, get back on the scales and generally ask someone else to re-read them - depending on the size of the dog it's not necessarily an easy task to hold the dog and read the scales at the same time.

Whenever you pick your dog up, ensure that you bend your knees and that you pick the dog up comfortably and support its full body while you do so. It is not good to pick a dog up by its front legs in the same manner as you may do with a child reaching up with its arms *(pictures above)*.

And if your dog is not able to be picked up and your local vet doesn't have scales, how about asking at the local post office or freight company - they generally have scales that are large and set low on the ground.

RECIPE 30

SPRAYING YOUR DOG

There are times when it may become necessary to use an aerosol or spray on your dog. In the breed show ring, the use of sprays to control the coat can be seen everywhere, however you may live in a hot climate that is susceptible to small biting insects that annoy both you and your dog, both insect and flea control can come in a spray formula.

Whatever reason you have to spray your dog it is important that the dog learns that it is acceptable and is comfortable with you doing so. Many dogs hate aerosols, the noise of the spray scares them and the smell is often overpowering for a dog.

- Have the dog standing with its face away furthest away from the spray.
- Always spray with the direction away from the head towards the tail.
- Start with the back legs and work backwards up the dog.
- Click and treat every time the spray is depressed, it may be easier to have someone else click and treating or spraying, while you do the other.
- If you need to administer the spray to the dog's head, ensure its eyes; nose; ears and mouth are properly covered. Spraying your hand, a cloth or brush and wiping around the head is much safer and more preferable than actually spraying the face.

7 Professional Grooming Salon

The biggest difference between the grooming of a dog at home or the grooming being done by a professional is often the time limitation. Many people find it much easier to take their dogs to a salon or even to have a mobile option come to their home, and as our lives get busier taking up the option to do this is definitely on the rise.

A professional is generally experienced in a wide variety of breeds and mixed breeds, deal with numerous sizes of dogs and come across a variety of wonderful and sometimes challenging personalities. This experience enables the professional to perform the grooming function more quickly even while still maintaining a positive relationship with the dog.

However because the professional is running a business it is difficult to establish good grooming behaviour from the dog, as often this is taught over a longer period of time than the groomer has available. As a professional I love grooming very young puppies because I know that I will teach them right from the start about having fun being groomed and that there is no need to stress. I will often talk to my client's owners about it first as I believe it is much more important that the puppy have a stress-free time and not necessarily have the greatest groom, than learn not to enjoy it but look perfect. If the pup is taught well and in a positive manner right from the start it will soon be calm, confident and comfortable having anything done to it and it is at that point where the perfect groom can be achieved.

But even the most salon cautious dog can learn to love the process, regardless of age they will learn. They may be more suspicious or wary but with respect and care will also prosper within the positive environment.

I have groomed many dogs that have obviously not had the best past experiences in the grooming parlour including ones that were often sedated to be groomed - I can quite confidently say that through the positive fun methods that I use that none of my clients are sedated anymore, most of them actually enjoy being groomed and some of them even come running. There are still one or two though who will just put up with being groomed but whether they admit it or not I know they walk away with more strut in their pace than when they arrived. And yes we still have the odd dog that unfortunately requires a muzzle as it nips first and asks questions later but even these ones will learn well using the positive clicker methods. I see dogs like this as a bigger training challenge; the muzzle has to be used in order to get the grooming task complete with minimal fuss to the dog.

PROFESSIONAL ENVIRONMENT APPLICATION

As a professional groomer I ensure that my methods are consistent, comfortable and relaxed. I perform each function in the same way and even though I can change the order of which I perform tasks, the methodology is constant. As I've said before, the dog's first language is that of the body - if you give off a relaxed and calm attitude and you perform functions in the same manner, the dogs quickly learn to read your body and anticipate the task.

I often talk to my clients throughout their groom; I try not to use a reassuring voice but one with interest and appeal. A voice that is calm will soothe a dog without praising it for nervousness. I praise the dogs throughout the groom when they offer wanted behaviour and I ignore any unwanted behaviours. I've seen many dogs groomed with correction and being told off is often the only communication they get during the process. I can see the amazement and confusion in some dogs when they get praise rather than correction, and it doesn't generally take any of them long to settle down and enjoy the new process.

If I know that I've got a dog coming in that needs extra work, then I will make the effort to schedule extra time, if I get stressed that I'm not working fast enough, then my client stresses out along with me - effectively the groom takes twice as long.

If as a professional you want to use food as a reward for a dog, then you must clear it with the owner first, ensuring that you tell them what type and brand of food you will be using. When I first started professionally the dogs only ever got a treat right at the end - it was (and still is for many) a wonderful effort to go through the average of an hour-long process for a tiny dog biscuit at the end. However I do believe the extra attention, kisses and cuddles that they receive at home is eventually associated directly with the grooming. The attention generally starts when their owners pick them up and this happens with us present - every time!

When using the clicker in the salon I will often use a clicker board rather than the hand clicker as it leaves me free to use both hands all of the time. When I get the opportunity to use food rewards throughout the groom then any good behaviour is accentuated and the unwanted behaviours diminish more quickly. Food rewards are more direct and efficient than other rewards and they can be administered fast. Play, verbal and tacit rewards are important but are often not consistent and can take time for the dog to understand amongst our other more complex babble of words and movements.

Imagine going to a place where all they do is pamper, massage and praise you!

Ah Bliss!

ABOUT THE AUTHOR

Karen McCarthy was given her first dog, a Gordon Setter when she was 12 years of age. Troy became a breed show dog and also worked in obedience training and it was the start of love that has Karen where she is today.

When Guinness came along (also a Gordon Setter) training took on a life of its own and Karen became hooked on obedience competitions. Then at her local club Central Allbreeds Dog Training School in Wellington, New Zealand, Karen began teaching others about the wonders of using positive reinforcement for training. Having Gordon Setters and trying to ask them to perform the same functions as other competing breeds while using the outdated style of corrective training just doesn't mix. Any dog can be a challenge to a trainer, but regardless of breed all of them absolutely love being clicker trained as the positive reinforcement gives them a beautiful attitude, a willingness to work and an ability to perform that can take them as far as it suits the handler.

Dogs have always been such a passion with Karen that she eventually bought a mobile dog grooming business, expanding that to include a salon with staff which took the passion to a whole new level. Karen also teaches puppy preschool classes and professional dog training classes at higher levels along with visiting clients on behaviour consultations as part of the ever-growing passion. Working as a groomer has given her an intimate insight into working with a variety of dogs both pedigrees and ones that are purely unique breeds.

Karen lives in Wellington, New Zealand with two different Gordon Setters, Connor and his daughter Vienna (plus a clicker trained cat). Connor is a retired breed show champion, but still competes actively in obedience, agility and heelwork to music. Vienna is still just starting out but is enthusiastic, a very quick learner and loves trying everything and missing out on nothing.

AUTHOR'S NOTE:

I hope you enjoy this book; it's been a work in progress (mostly in my head while I work) for about 4 years. I'd like to thank all the hundreds of dogs that have taught me about behaviour while grooming and training and also to Kay Laurence for having the confidence in me to put this together. I'd also like to say a special thank you to my colleagues and friends in the dog world who helped me onto the wonderful track of clicker training - and specially to Guinness who taught me how positive reinforcement training has more benefits than just for learning behaviour.

Made in the USA
Monee, IL
08 May 2025

16989787R00050